# CRITICAL THINKING IN A NUTSHELL

HOW TO BECOME AN INDEPENDENT THINKER
AND MAKE INTELLIGENT DECISIONS

THINKNETIC

# GET 2 FREE BOOKLETS!

## Astute Tools To Sharpen Your Thinking, Become Wiser & Make Smarter Decisions

A glimpse into what you'll discover inside:

- If your thinking is flawed and what it takes to fix it (the solutions are included)
- Simple and effective strategies to make sound and regret-free decisions
- Tried and true hacks to elevate your rationality and change your live for the better
- Enlightening principles to guide your thoughts and actions (gathered from the wisest man of all time)

**Go to thinknetic.net to download for free!**

(Or simply scan the code with your camera)

# CONTENTS

*Introduction*   vii

1. What Is Critical Thinking?   1
2. Critical Thinking Framework: Understanding The Elements And Steps Needed For Critical Thinking   15
3. The Evolution Of A Critical Mind: What Sets Critical Thinkers Apart   41
4. Barriers To Critical Thinking   57
5. Ready, Set, Go: Applying Critical Thinking To Your Personal And Professional Life   73
6. Simple And Fun Mental Exercises To Develop And Practice Critical Thinking   95

*Afterword*   107
*One Final Word From Us*   110
*Continuing Your Journey*   113
*The Team Behind Thinknetic*   115
*References*   119
*Disclaimer*   123

# INTRODUCTION

You have a task to resolve at work. You know that to resolve the problem, so much would need to change. You toy with the possibility of coming up with a far-reaching plan to solve the real fundamental issue at stake.

But you know it is impractical. You do not have the time or energy to challenge the status quo. You know you will face opposition from other people. Therefore, you end up making a solid plan. But one which will not make too many waves or provide the necessary change. However, you can't shake a feeling of dissatisfaction as you make this uninspiring plan.

Do you ever have a nagging feeling that you could be doing things better? That your brain is capable of so much more than small mind-numbing tasks? Do you have great ideas but do not always have the time or energy to follow through?

You want to do your best at your job and life, but there are too many competing pressures on your time. It is hard to know where to start, and sometimes it seems much easier just to do the minimum.

You may have heard that critical thinking is an essential skill in today's workplace. Most employers say that they look for candidates with these skills and are hard-pressed to find them. Every school curriculum focuses on how to cultivate these skills.

Critical thinking has become a corporate buzzword, like synergy or core competency. However, unlike those empty words, critical thought represents a proven tradition of deep understanding and problem solving, which has advanced our society immeasurably. Science, technology, and philosophy would all be impossible without it.

You may also think that critical thinking is time-consuming. Who has time to sit and ponder every single decision? You are 100% correct.

It is impractical and utterly a waste of time to use the full force of critical thought for every minor decision you make. However, when you are making an important decision, employing critical thinking will not only make it far more likely that you make a correct decision, it will also save you time.

The skills honed in critical thought will give you the foresight to predict and prepare in advance for time-wasting problems. Nothing saves more time than getting things right the first time.

I plan to inspire you on this journey. I have been an educator for well over a decade and spent many more years in private and government positions. I also have a Ph.D. in political science. But more importantly, I have a firm personal commitment to clear and purposeful thought exemplified by many years of training students and employees. I hope my passion for the topic comes through in this book.

Are you prepared to understand the world better? Are you ready to create new and better solutions to the problems in your life? Join me in discovering how to master critical thinking skills to jump-start positive changes in your life. Together we can unleash the power of critical thinking by reading this book.

# 1
# WHAT IS CRITICAL THINKING?

**The Death Of Socrates**

The leaders of Athens sentenced the greatest mind of his generation to death. Socrates was to ingest hemlock. A horrific way to die. The philosopher's entire body would become paralyzed before his bladder would be overwhelmed by toxicity. Socrates would experience frothing at the mouth and respiratory distress. Finally, a massive seizure would lead to death.

Many accused Socrates of "not believing the Gods of the city, introducing new gods, and corrupting the youth" [1]. In his informal role as educator, Socrates had taught many of the youngest and brightest to question all assumptions. He taught them ideas were not necessarily correct, just because their parents or leaders said it was so. Socrates told his students to examine every idea on its merits alone.

Though accused of undermining authority, Socrates never supported rebellion for its own sake. Instead, he insisted that the ideas dispensed by people in positions of authority were not above question. Rather than defend a certain power structure, Socrates taught his students to seek out the truth. Though Socrates died, his students Plato and Aristotle carried this tradition forward. The man was dead, but his legacy remains immortal [2].

The method of inquiry he pioneered is still known as the Socratic Method, and it focuses on the development of ideas through constant dialogue. Each argument is teased out and broken down into its underlying assumptions. Each assumption is exposed to ruthless scrutiny no matter who made them and why [3].

The trial of Socrates emphasizes the power of questioning established sources of authority and information. On the one hand, the powers that decided to end the philosopher's life. On the other, the thought of Socrates inspired a long-standing tradition [4].

Critical thinking is an essential component of human progress. Without questioning authority and common wisdom, the science and progress we have today would be impossible. The study of evolution would be impossible if scientists were unwilling to challenge the Bible's literal interpretation. What if we still believed the world was flat? Or that Kings enjoy a divine right to rule?

Critical thinking skills are among the most sought after in the modern economy. In a major survey of American business leaders, 93% of respondents agreed with the statement that "a demonstrated capacity to think critically, communicate clearly, and solve complex problems is more important than [a candidate's] undergraduate major" [5]. By becoming more critical thinkers, we become more well-rounded people. It doesn't hurt that we become more employable on the way, too [6]!

**How To Define Critical Thinking**

When people use the term critical thinking, it can mean different things. However, certain elements are essential for a fuller understanding of the concept.

The Delphi Project provided one of the best-known definitions of the term:

"Purposeful, self-regulatory judgment which results in interpretation, analysis, evaluation, and inference, as well as an explanation of the evidential, conceptual, methodological, criteriological, or contextual considerations upon which that judgment is based"[7].

A good translation of this definition into layman's terms would be the ability to think about connected ideas thoroughly and independently, basing those ideas on factual evidence. It is the act of turning the full force of our reasoning towards resolving real-world problems.

How is this done? Critical thinkers gather and categorize evidence data relevant to their problem to gain relevant knowledge. As different elements of the problem and its potential solution are understood, critical thinkers connect an issue's disparate parts into one workable framework.

Once a critical thinker has analyzed the problem, dividing it into digestible definitions and categories, will then use this knowledge to solve the problem.

They then make the connections necessary to understand and define the problem and all of its components.

Another approach to defining critical thinking is to look at what it isn't. The word critical can throw people off. This is not an approach designed to criticize things we don't like. You know that person at work you don't like? Ever notice how every time they talk, you try to find something wrong with their ideas? That isn't critical thinking. That's just being critical.

Critical thinking is not a more methodical way of defending ideas we agree with. Sometimes when we argue, we brilliantly defend our position, assuming that everything the other side says is wrong. You can see this happen in just about every argument held on social media. When we use our intellect to prove a point we have not thought through, we are not thinking critically, no matter how well we do it.

We often try to make ideas look better or worse than they are for our own gain. This is not critical thinking.

A critical thinker is only interested in evaluating the strength of an argument as it is without exaggerating reality in either direction. When we apply critical thinking, we attempt to treat arguments we like and dislike objectively and fairly.

## What Is Critical Thinking Good For?

When you engage in critical thinking, your purpose is to attain one thing only: the truth. Your pursuit of truth means that you can avoid deception and identify which facts are accurate. This is because you will now know how to separate facts from spin, allowing you to arrive at true solutions [8].

Does it sometimes seem like the world around you is operating wrong? Do you ever ask yourself why you encounter so many disorganized and inefficient systems? Have you ever thought that given a chance, you could do things better?

You probably can. We encounter incompetence and inefficiency, far too often. To a great extent, this is because we don't question existing traditions and processes. Existing systems are usually not the product of design. Instead, outdated social beliefs, cultural norms, and simple inertia shape the systems we encounter. People in authority tell us what to believe, and far too often, we accept the common wisdom.

Critical thinking provides us with the tools to cut through that. From problems as small as where to go on vacation to large ones, such as who to marry, critical thinking allows us to make better decisions.

These skills are essential in the current economy, with its emphasis on start-ups and entrepreneurship. Tech companies champion an approach of "disruptive innovation"[9]. They attempt to create new markets and value systems, which displace existing business models. A disruptive plan is an exercise in critical thinking. To replace a current model, you will first examine it and assess its weaknesses and strengths. Next, you will design a more efficient plan, disregarding traditional "common sense" models.

Amazon took over the book market by disrupting the traditional marketplace. Bookstores remained beloved institutions, and it was still commonplace to go to a store to sell or buy a book. Nonetheless, this traditional business model suffered severe drawbacks. There was a good chance that some books that customers wanted were unavailable because of limited shelf space. Prices were high due to significant overhead expenses. Finally, bookstores were unable to expose their customers to information on new books efficiently.

Amazon.com revolutionized book sales by coming to the business from the outside. Jeff Bezos, the entrepreneur behind the company, was disinterested in maintaining tradition. Instead, his mission was to use the internet to provide services efficiently. Only after researching several inefficient industries did he decide to enter the book business.

He chose to sell books rather than other products since customers did not have to try them or taste them. They were well suited for remote purchases. As unpleasant as this may sound, from a business perspective, bookstores were rendered unnecessary.

Having reached this conclusion, Bezos designed a system that would overcome the flaws of the bookstore model. The information delivery problem was overcome by centering recommendations and reviews on the website homepage. Amazon overcame stocking problems by storing books in massive delivery centers across the country. Meanwhile, it lowered prices by stocking up in bulk and paying less overhead [10].

What Jeff Bezos designed was a simple and intuitive solution to long-standing problems in the traditional industry. What made it revolutionary was that it ignored the value system and common wisdom of the book industry. Instead, Bezos examined each of the assumptions underlying the industry critically. Amazon.com is the product of critical thinking, a very profitable and successful one.

### What Does Critical Thinking Consist Of?

The process of critical thinking involves recurring concepts and components.

Perception: Our first step to thinking about anything is to perceive the situation. We cannot be aware of a problem that requires solving unless we have perceived it first. It is important to keep in mind that our perception is not objective or neutral. Our perception is how we filter objective reality through our subjective value systems.

For example, let's say you are setting up your monthly budget. You may find that you are unable to save a substantial amount of money. However, your parents instilled in you the importance of saving money. You may see this as a serious problem with your budgeting. If you live one day at a time, you may shrug your shoulders and say, "thank goodness I have enough!"

Assumptions: Our assumptions are unexamined beliefs taken for granted. Our plans and actions are, usually unknowingly, built on assumptions. To foster critical thinking, we must be willing to examine our assumptions critically to see if they are accurate and serve a practical purpose. Remember, you cannot assume anything is true unless you have reviewed it thoroughly.

Going back to our previous example, neither tendency is necessarily the correct one. Examine them carefully. If you are going to actively decrease your budget in the future, you may not need to squeeze every penny. If your current budget is a long-term one, not saving anything can be a serious problem. Whatever your beliefs are on saving, examine how relevant they are to your current situation.

Emotions: Many people believe that rational thought is impossible unless you put your emotions aside. This is neither true nor realistic. Instead, emotions are an integral part of the critical thinking process. As human beings, we are highly emotional, and our natural feelings color and influence every decision we make. This is not a bad thing.

We can use our critical thinking skills to improve the world around us. There is no way to do that without using emotional indicators. For example, solving problems in our children's lives is a noble and worthy goal for rational thought. However, it is meaningless without the emotional significance of parenthood and the institution of the family. Do not be afraid to use emotional attachments and indicators to determine what problems you wish to solve and how.

<u>Language:</u> The words we use are the nuts and bolts of critical thinking. We can turn our thoughts from vague concepts into firm ones by applying precise language to the problem. To think critically about any topic, we have to define the problem and our approach to solving it in an actionable manner. Critical thinking is only possible when we make an abstract representation of reality through words.

Going back to our budgeting example, to unpack how much money we need to save, there are several concepts we need to take into account, for example, inflation. Sure, our budget may be enough for right now. But will it be in the future? How likely do prices rise? Correspondingly, to calculate how much we need to save, we have to understand the concept of interest. Putting the relevant factors into words and concepts helps us understand the problems we face.

Arguments: In the context of critical thought, the word argument is a crucial building block. It does not refer to people disagreeing with each other loudly. Instead, it is a well-reasoned list of assumptions and premises. When these assumptions formulate an argument, they result in a functional and rational conclusion. As we already discussed, we back up logical assumptions with logic and facts. Otherwise, we could be formulating conclusions based on faulty logic [11].

Fallacies: Consistent human tendencies towards uncritical thinking are known as "fallacies." A fallacy is a belief or conclusion reached through unsound logic. It is an argument or belief that will not stand up to critical scrutiny. Though a fallacy may not be wrong, it is by definition based on an illogical thought process.

Applying fallacies in your thought process increases your chances of reaching the wrong conclusion. However, life isn't that straightforward. Sometimes a fallacy ridden thought process can achieve outstanding results. Remember that old saying, "even a broken clock is right twice a day?" That is what it means.

For example, imagine you are eating a bag of assorted jelly beans. Your friend says to you, "I bet you $100 the next one you take out of the bag is green." When you ask why, the friend explains, "The last jelly bean you ate was green, and therefore all jelly beans are green." You argue but take the bet. The next jelly bean you withdraw is, yup, you guessed it, green. Your friend says, "see!" In this case, your friend's logic was faulty, but he was right. That is an extreme case. But often, fallacies seem logical and even clever arguments [12].

Logic: This is a word for structured thinking, designed to evaluate information accurately. By analyzing the premises and assumptions' validity, a critical thinker can distinguish between fallacies and strong assumptions, thus between truth and falsehood. If we are logical, we will replace a false premise or assumption with a valid one [13].

For example, let's say we only save 10$ a month. We may panic and think that we will always be living hand-to-mouth and think we need to make significant changes in our employment or living situation. However, a logical look at our budget might reveal this is not true. If, for example, we pay $500 a month on our student loans, and next month is the last payment, we may soon be saving $510 a month! Applying a logical outlook to all the available information may change our overall evaluation of the problem.

Problem Solving: Critical thinking in the abstract may be interesting, but it does not make the world around us better. We usually apply these time-consuming skills when confronted with a severe problem in need of resolution. Finding a better way of approaching a problem or achieving a goal means little unless you take steps to apply it practically [14].

## Action Steps

Let's perform an exercise and see what role critical thinking has played in your life so far and how you can apply it in the future.

Take one of the most significant and most difficult decisions you have made in your life. Maybe moving to another state or country, marrying or breaking up with a significant other, or quitting a job. It doesn't matter as long as you had options, and it wasn't easy to choose between them.

Next, do the following:

1. Write down all the alternatives you had to the decision ultimately made.
2. Write down why you choose one over the other.
3. Were these reasons based on facts you thoroughly researched or on assumptions?
4. What assumptions informed that decision?
5. How do you know these assumptions to be true? Have you examined their validity?
6. Do you make many of your decisions based on unfounded assumptions? What are some examples?

When we make decisions, we make many unproven assumptions. Sometimes they are the product of our upbringing or beliefs. For example, in American society, we are taught to pay our debts and emphasize self-sufficiency. This cultural inclination influences some individuals to continue to accrue debts they can't pay even though filing for bankruptcy would be a much better option.

Maybe these ideas were imparted to us by an authority figure. Half the time, we don't even know where they come from. Although it is completely normal to make unfounded assumptions, this tendency can have negative repercussions. It may mean we are making bad decisions based on faulty information.

The good news is that it isn't so hard to fix the problem. When we make an important decision, it is worth taking time to examine our assumptions and act based on accurate information and valid arguments. Yes, it involves a bit of extra work. But after all, Socrates died for his right to question falsehoods. Don't we owe him a little extra effort?

## 2
# CRITICAL THINKING FRAMEWORK: UNDERSTANDING THE ELEMENTS AND STEPS NEEDED FOR CRITICAL THINKING

In 1974, Sony executives were optimistic about producing a superior product, and they were right. The executives told their technicians they wanted to record anything on TV at the highest level of quality available on the market. The lab team produced a product that no other company could compete with called "Betamax."

Sony believed that if they rushed the release of their superior product before their rivals could release anything comparable, then "Betamax" would ultimately control the market. This worked, and Sony had the market completely cornered.

Hoping to capitalize quickly on this advantage, the Sony executives neglected some important problems with their product. Betamax had to contend that its cassettes could only contain one hour's worth of programming. This turned out to be a consequential mistake.

Imagine you had to attend a boring PTA meeting that coincided with the screening of "The Godfather." If you wanted to record it on TV, the Betamax tape would record only the first hour. Sure, you would get the wedding scene in beautiful color. But you would miss Sonny's assassination and horse head scene!

Meanwhile, the executives at JVS tried a different approach. They had already lost market control. Their best recourse was to examine the Betamax system for flaws. Knowing that they could not rival Sony for picture quality, JVS simply released a tape with a longer recording duration.

This flaw was responsible for Sony losing its complete control over home consumer video products within a few quick years. While Betamax controlled 100% of the market in 1975, by 1980, JVC had a 60% share. Sony failed to deliver the kind of product that fulfilled customer needs.

To make matters worse, Sony never adapted. They continued to focus primarily on picture quality over the duration, believing they had a comparative advantage in that metric. They maintained their visual superiority, hoping to regain the market by increasing the length of tapes somewhat. They also refused to discontinue the line. By the late 1980s, Sony had wholly lost its market share despite continued production of Betamax tapes until 2016(!), long after the brand had become a marketing joke.

What did Sony get wrong? Their plan was flawed. A strong idea is successful if fitted into a strong strategy. Although you may view critical thinking as thinking deeply about something, it is more accurate to imagine it as a series of steps. Critical thought is a process, not an event.

In this chapter, we will examine the elements and process of critical thinking deeply and systematically. First, we will look at the Paul-Elder framework, which provides an overview of the main elements that go into critical thinking. Then we will examine Bloom's Taxonomy, an approach that maps out the process of critical thinking from inception to the creation of solutions to real-life problems. Finally, we will see how these theoretical frameworks apply to decisions in your life.

**The Paul-Elder Framework**

We have talked about the elements of critical thinking and their importance. But how do we apply its principles to real-life problems? In the 1990s, educational scientist Linda Elder, and the Director of Research at the Center for Critical Thinking Richard Paul, created a process for developing critical thinking. It remains the most advanced and widely recognized blueprint for the critical thought process [1].

Paul and Elder's framework has three sections: reasoning, intellectual standards, and intellectual traits. The intellectual traits section deals with the personality traits associated with critical thought. Paul and Elder believe that if these traits are actively encouraged in education, it will raise individuals able to calmly and successfully process and solve even the most complex problems. These include the following:

- Intellectual humility
- Intellectual courage
- Intellectual empathy
- Intellectual autonomy
- Intellectual integrity
- Intellectual perseverance
- Confidence in reason
- Fair-mindedness

Meanwhile, the intellectual standards section deals with the technical manner in which we analyze data and build our arguments. These elements are important in the practical process of pursuing critical thought. When we appraise our own thought process and others' thought process, we should measure it by these standards. A serious flaw in any of these standards increases the odds of a flawed process and outcome.

A true process of critical thinking will comply with high levels of each of the following standards:

- Clarity
- Accuracy
- Precision
- Relevance

- Depth
- Breadth
- Logic
- Significance
- Fairness

We will return to these elements in-depth later in the book to deal with the more practical critical thought elements.

First, let's look at the building blocks of the critical thought process. This is the focus of the elements of reasoning in the Paul-Elder framework. To better understand how to apply critical thinking to actual problems, we will use these elements to solve problems that commonly arise in the workplace.

<u>Elements of Reasoning</u>: This is where the Paul-Elder framework gets into the nuts and bolts of the process of critical thought. Reasoning is the act of thinking an issue through, logically and clearly, while drawing well-founded inferences and conclusions on the matter. As you can see from the description, this is a structured process. I suggest that when you actively approach a significant problem, you conduct each one of the elements in the sequence, moving on to the next only when completing the previous one.

How do we apply a process of reasoning to real-life problems? We use thought to solve all of our problems. However, most of our thoughts are random and fleeting.

Our mind tends to produce thoughts that are neither critical nor useful.

According to the Paul-Elder framework, critical thinking differs from other forms of thought.

The Paul-Elder framework suggests we pay attention to specific thought elements. By focusing on these elements, we can dig deeper and reach reasonable and practical conclusions.

*Purpose*: All reasoning strives for something clear and specific. Instead of fleeting observations, we are looking to reach a productive and concrete end.

*Problem-solving*: The purpose of our critical thought should be to resolve a problem. Critical thought is an involved and complex process. It is best used to make our lives and the world better by resolving a hindrance to progress.

*Assumptions*: We have concrete assumptions about the world. If we have to reinvent the wheel every time we analyze a phenomenon, it is hard to build a solid foundation of thought. We have to be careful which assumptions we make, but ultimately there are certain things we simply assume to be true. Keep unexamined assumptions to a necessary minimum. For example, let's say your boss asks you to develop a plan to increase stockholders' revenue. You want to keep your job; therefore, you will assume that the capitalist system functions and you wish to be a part of it.

*Point of view*: Humans are not even remotely neutral. We derive many of our thought patterns from our culture, biases, and self-interested viewpoints. Our reasoning process is no exception. The important part is to be aware of our biases.

*Data*: When we think critically, we back up our assumptions and conclusions with data. Remember, reliable data is the best antidote to our biases and wishful thinking.

*Interpretation of data*: We interpret our data and findings to create a well-founded narrative. This is a careful balancing act. Data and facts do not speak for themselves. Therefore, we need to tell a purposeful story based on what we have found (e.g., well-researched, non-fiction story). We can't make the facts say anything that doesn't appear in the data, and we cannot assume missing data confirms our biases.

*Concepts and Language*: We express this narrative in a communicable manner that is readily understood by our audience. We do not sacrifice the veracity of our facts to communicate them.

*Implications and consequences*: In the first part of the framework, we devised a purpose for our thought process. Here we make sure that our efforts have fulfilled that purpose. We take all of the hard work we put in and use it to address the problem at hand [2].

## Applying The Paul-Elder Framework

Bethany, a hard-working and fair-minded boss at a marketing firm, was in charge of a very talented staff. However, there has been disquiet recently.

Shawn is the best performer on Bethany's team, but he does not get along with his co-workers. Unfortunately, he is an arrogant and obnoxious individual.

If the boss in our story were to follow the Paul-Elder framework, what major elements will go into her decision?

Purpose: Bethany has a problem: her success has always come from balancing productivity with her staff's cohesion and morale. She believes that Shawn's behavior risks that balance.

Assumptions: Bethany has her own unexamined but deeply believed assumptions on how to succeed professionally. She feels that teamwork and a pleasant and collegial working atmosphere are critical for productivity. As a corollary to this, she believes the encouragement of individual achievement at the expense of group cohesion is immoral and impractical.

Shawn's self-centered approach has always concerned her despite his achievements. Therefore, she was not remotely surprised when problems emerged on that front. Due to her assumptions and orientation, she believes the other team members' resentment is completely justified.

Point of view: Bethany maintains a highly professional demeanor at all times and rarely reveals her biases. However, she has them. Her emotional commitment to her team and their welfare is what makes Bethany a great boss. She goes the extra mile for her staff, and they repay her with excellent work.

For the same reason, she has difficulty dealing with Shawn rationally. He drives her nuts. When she tried to talk to him, he told her that he would continue acting as he always does because it gets results and he is irreplaceable. This made her so angry; she almost fired him on the spot.

If she had done so, she would have made a crucial decision without weighing the pros and cons. However, she managed to control herself and continued to pursue a process of reasoning.

Communication through language: Bethany imagined him as harmful bacteria attacking the healthy body of her team. When envisioned that way, the only solution in her mind was to fire Shawn.

But as a smart boss, Bethany knew this approach was irrational. So, she wrote down what problem she was attempting to solve and why. Putting down her purpose in precise and unambiguous language, she came up with two primary goals: maintaining group morale and promoting high productivity. By using precise language, Bethany reminded herself that her goal was not to get rid of

Shawn. It was still an option, but it would be a means to an end.

<u>Backing Arguments Up with Data</u>: Bethany tried to construct a written argument for firing Shawn. She firmly believed that terminating him would make the group happier and more cohesive. After all, before Shawn's head got inflated, everyone got along better. The atmosphere in the break room was healthier. This was a fact, and she was confident in its validity.

However, it was harder for Bethany to make an argument that his dismissal would improve productivity. She decided to test her assumptions and look at the raw data of her team's performance, and see what she could learn from trends in productivity before and after Shawn changed his attitude for the worse.

A thorough review of the numbers indicated that the bad atmosphere had not lowered productivity. Not only had Shawn's productivity increased sharply in recent months, but everyone else was doing better as well. This went against Bethany's preconceptions and made her feel very unpleasant and aggravated.

<u>Interpretation of data</u>: The data Bethany had compiled did not match her preconceptions. Yes, the cohesion of the group had suffered as a result of Shawn's behavior. But somehow, productivity was up. Why?

Then it hit her. These numbers could only mean one thing: Shawn's annoying behavior motivated the other employees to put him in his place. The ensuing sense of competition had inspired everyone to work harder.

Bethany did not like this result, but that was the most coherent story she could make out of these numbers.

Between Shawn's exemplary numbers and the fierce attempts of others in the group to compete with him, productivity had increased. On a rational level, she could not justify firing Shawn. At least not over productivity.

It turned out that she had been operating based on a fallacy. Her deep personal commitment to team spirit and her belief in the importance of workplace morale shaped her views on productivity. Her firm belief was that if the team does not work as a group, productivity and work quality will suffer. This was a fair assumption. However, the facts do not back it up.

Implications and Consequences: Bethany did not engage in this taxing mental exercise for fun. She did it to improve her team's morale and productivity. So she took the data she had amassed and her interpretation of it and fashioned it into a plan.

She discovered that some competition between the members of her team increased overall productivity. Therefore, she abandoned her faulty premise that competition and a focus on personal achievement were inherently destructive.

Meanwhile, she had used evidence to substantiate her assumption that Shawn's behavior disturbed the group's harmony. Therefore, she still needed to fix that problem. Her logic told her that she had to find a way to foster her team's competitive instincts while maintaining her workers' morale.

The data showed a mixed picture. It was clear that Shawn's behavior benefitted the group in some ways while harming it in others. Therefore, the logical thing to do was to maximize the benefit and decrease the harm caused by his presence [3].

Bethany developed a plan to designate tasks that complimented each worker's strength. Shawn was given a new title and placed separately from the other workers. Bethany gave Shawn tasks that matched his lone-wolf style. Meanwhile, Bethany gave the other team members tasks better suited for collaborative efforts.

The plan minimized interaction between Shawn and the other workers. However, at the end of the month, all workers would participate in a productivity evaluation meeting. This would foster a useful spirit of competition without unduly disrupting group harmony. By using critical thinking, Bethany had resolved the problem without compromising group productivity.

**Bloom's Taxonomy**

As we saw in this example, critical thinking is a process and not an event. But what exactly is that process, and how does one stage flow into another? Since critical thinking is a deliberate and structured process, the order in which we go about it is important. Bloom's Taxonomy is the most commonly used blueprint of critical thought. In the 1940s, a committee of educators tasked with promoting critical thinking imagined this as a pyramid, with different forms of thought building on each other. The result remains highly influential today [4].

**Bloom's Taxonomy**

- **create**: Produce new or original work
  Design, assemble, construct, conjecture, develop, formulate, author, investigate
- **evaluate**: Justify a stand or decision
  appraise, argue, defend, judge, select, support, value, critique, weigh
- **analyze**: Draw connections among ideas
  differentiate, organize, relate, compare, contrast, distinguish, examine, experiment, question, test
- **apply**: Use information in new situations
  execute, implement, solve, use, demonstrate, interpret, operate, schedule, sketch
- **understand**: Explain ideas or concepts
  classify, describe, discuss, explain, identify, locate, recognize, report, select, translate
- **remember**: Recall facts and basic concepts
  define, duplicate, list, memorize, repeat, state

Vanderbilt University Center for Teaching

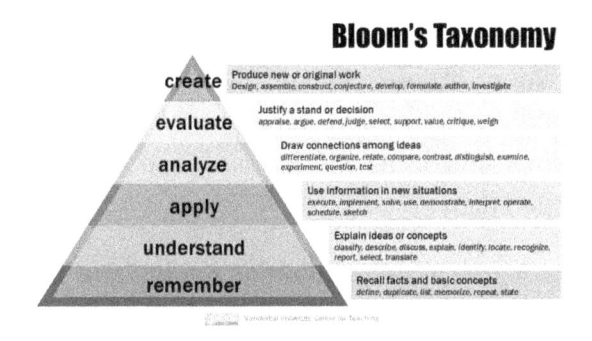

Figure 1. Bloom's Taxonomy Pyramid illustrates the connection between each step. Image generously shared by the Vanderbilt Center for Teaching.

Figure 1 above shows the Bloom Taxonomy pyramid after its revision in 2001. The two versions are mostly similar, but there are some differences. Most notably, in the old version, the evaluate step was the highest level of the pyramid. However, the 2001 update established the create step as the new highest category [5].

Bloom's pyramid presents a practical path to innovation through critical thinking. It reminds us of two important facts. First, that genuine critical thought is hard work! There are several steps we need to take, and each one can be challenging. Second, if you do the hard work, you can create something genuinely new and exciting [6].

Bloom's taxonomy is a practical scheme with each step building on the previous one. Therefore, we will put it to the test on a real-life problem.

In 2004, the documentary "Super Size Me" was released. The creator of the documentary ate nothing but McDonald's menu items three times a day. Viewers watched in horror as his physical and mental health deteriorated daily.

This was a public image disaster for the world's largest fast-food restaurant chain. Unhealthy and obese customers sued McDonald's for damages, and sales plummeted.

As Americans became increasingly aware of the importance of maintaining a healthy lifestyle, McDonald's image for fast and unhealthy food was becoming a hindrance. Many consumers associated McDonald's with obesity and heart disease in their minds.

The company announced an effort at complete rebranding to turn McDonald's into "a more trusted and respectable brand."

Within a few years, McDonald's turned around its image and restored profits to its previous levels and beyond. How did they do so?

The company announced an 18-month strategy to overhaul the brand completely.

What steps did McDonald's have to take to revitalize its brand?

Remember: When engaging in problem-solving, the first step is to remember relevant forms and sources of information. These can include facts, concepts, terms, or sources of information you know, such as books or websites.

In this stage, McDonald's looked at the raw data to handle the market's current needs. This included running focus groups with consumers.

They also gathered their sales data from the last few years, but that would not be enough. McDonald's even examined some of their rivals' relative success, which involved their immediate fast-food competitors and other food and beverage chains. This approach gave McDonald's a better understanding of the contemporary market. For example, they examined the approaches of competitors such as Chipotle, which had grown quickly.

Understand: Once you have the relevant materials, study them until you feel you have a full understanding of the issue at hand. Whether you are an expert on the topic or only have a basic grasp of it, this is a necessary step. Do not move on until you feel you can explain all the important facts, concepts, and terms you have remembered. You cannot apply the information when you don't understand it.

One good metric for understanding is your ability to explain a concept in the absolute simplest terms. As

Albert Einstein, the brilliant theoretical physicist, famously put it, "If you can't explain it to a six-year-old, you don't understand it yourself."

As we have discussed previously, data does not speak for itself. Looking over it, McDonald's executives discovered two trends in sales. Companies that stressed the health benefits of their products tended to increase revenues. Also, customers now reported that the atmosphere in the locations had become increasingly important to them.

Unfortunately, the association of the McDonald's brand with these fashionable elements was unsuccessful. The focus groups showed that the brand brought to mind cheap, unhealthy food, and their locations reminded people of screaming children and exploited employees.

<u>Apply</u>: Once you understand the problem, look at the knowledge you gathered while working through the two first rungs of Bloom's fine pyramid. Ask yourself the following questions?

- How does the knowledge <u>apply</u> to the question at hand?
- What is the most useful information for tackling this problem? What has been the least valuable?
- Is there knowledge you are missing, which could help you understand the problem better? If you miss significant information, you may want to go back to the previous step before continuing.

Analyze: Now you are ready to apply analysis to the problem. Break the problem into its parts. What are the major elements of the problem? Define them carefully. Once you have done this to your satisfaction, examine the links between the components. How does one influence the other? Why? What is motivating different actors to act in the way they do? Make sure you have a full working understanding of what the problem consists of and how it manifests.

To avoid distractions and noise, boil the logic behind your terms to the lowest number of assumptions possible. When we cannot determine between two explanations, it is better to prefer the simpler explanation. This principle is known as "Occam's Razor," referring to the philosopher William of Ockham, an English thinker known for "shaving away" unnecessary elements in arguments [7].

At this point, McDonald's executives were aware that their company's image as a purveyor of unhealthy food was very serious. The data suggested that chains and purveyors with a reputation for providing healthy food were fairing far better in the marketplace than those who do not.

Evaluate: You have done some good work to get to this point. Your work may look gorgeous on paper, with aesthetically pleasing diagrams and charts. When you have worked hard on a project, it is easy to get emotionally attached to your work. Avoid that trap.

Instead, ruthlessly subject it to criticism. Remember, if you don't, other people will. If there are any significant flaws in your analysis, reality will unapologetically reveal them.

Look at your analysis carefully and evaluate it according to the two metrics described below. If you find any flaws, now is the appropriate time to fix them.

1. Do they make sense internally? Based on your research in the earlier steps: does every definition stand up to scrutiny? Are you sure about the connections you have made, or are you guessing? How confident are you that your analysis is accurate and makes sense?

2. Do they make sense externally? The relevant question here is, are there sources of information external to your analysis that could invalidate key claims? Are there important sources of information you haven't looked at? Is there information you examined but did not take into account? Put yourself in the shoes of an expert on the topic. Would they say you are missing anything important?

McDonald's executives now asked themselves why they had such an insistent reputation for selling unhealthy products. Returning to their consumer focus groups, they realized that as the best known fast-food restaurant globally, all the industry's ills had tarnished them. Paradoxically, their iconic symbols, the golden arches, and its red background had become more infamous than famous.

Analyze: This is where you start to formulate a solution to the problem. When we analyze, we attempt to arrive at an approach superior to the current state of affairs.

We put our ideas into an actionable step-by-step plan. Make sure every step is realistic and deliverable. Then, subject it to the same tests you used to check the validity of your analysis. Does it make sense internally? Will any external circumstances change it?

Make sure your plan is realistic. Remember: despite the somewhat misleading name, problem-solving does not require eliminating the issue. It can just refer to a better way to do things. The great French Philosopher Voltaire once wrote, "perfection is the enemy of good." Once you have reached a good and useful plan which will improve things significantly, examine it to look for room to improve. But at some point, stop and put it into action. We must actively put our plans to the test.

McDonald's faced some serious dilemmas to improve its image. Their colors and arches were world-famous. Yet, they were driving customers away. Their Big Macs were legendary, yet increasingly unpopular.

Realizing a full change of image required a serious makeover, the executives at McDonald's changed the entire chain's aesthetic appeal. The company replaced the old shiny packing with recyclable packaging designed by students at the Miami International University of Art and Design. McDonald's redecorated their locations in green and brown earth tones. By doing so, the

McDonald's brass hoped to change the image of the brand.

<u>Synthesize</u>: At this stage, we take all of the elements we have arrived at and unite them into one plan. We make sure that our conclusions stand and that our plan to address them is valid and practical. We learn from mistakes we have made in previous steps and prepare to put our plan into action.

It was not enough for McDonald's to change the decor and iconography of the corporation. They had to address the menu itself for their image to change radically. The new menu emphasized new items such as salads and designer coffee. The new menu also highlighted each item's calorie value in a bid to increase dietary transparency.

The result transformed the somewhat cheap atmosphere of old McDonald's into a more pleasant and healthy-looking location.

<u>Create</u>: At the end of the long process of planning, we unleash our plan. The strands of our arguments and analysis come together into an actionable plan. As we put the plan into action, we watch to see how it fares in reality. Sometimes we need to readjust even the best-laid plans. Therefore, even when we put our plans into motion, we should view them as "works in progress," improving them, we receive new data.

McDonald's launched its new plan to great fanfare. They invited reporters and critics to a chef catered gala dinner, incorporating parts of their new menu. The next day they opened their key remodeled locations.

The improvement to its image was substantial. Profits rose as the plan softened the image of the chain.

**Action Steps**

Let's use these two models of critical thinking and apply them to a real problem in your life. This will benefit you in two ways. It will sharpen your understanding of the critical thought process and, if you do the process well, help you improve your day to day life.

Take a long and honest look at your health. Do you face any health conditions? What are your vitals in terms of blood pressure, blood pressure, cholesterol, etc.?

Look at your daily habits. Are you getting enough sleep? How is your diet? Do you get exercise, and if so, how often? How is your mental health? Make a genuine account of your normal daily schedule.

**Applying The Frameworks To Your Health**

Now that you have analyzed your health and lifestyle let's look at it again with the tools provided in this chapter.

Using the Paul-Elder Framework, analyze your daily schedule. Be brutally honest. Don't sugarcoat your mistakes. Write down your answers:

Purpose: Is the improvement of your health a major goal in your day to day life? If so, how does it shape your day? If not, why not? Should that change?

Problem-solving: What are the biggest obstacles in achieving robust health? How does your daily schedule help you overcome them? Should or could you be doing more?

Assumptions: In your health approach, do you make subconscious or conscious assumptions that you do not challenge? Should you challenge them?

Look in particular at your assumptions on the role of exercise, sleep, diet, medication, and work in your life. Are they all well examined?

Point-of-view: Do you have strong opinions on health-related matters? For example, are you a big fan of alternative medicine, or do you rely on pharmacology to get results? Were you raised to feel a certain way about food, drugs, alcohol, exercise, work-life balance? Does that influence your lifestyle and your health?

Data and corroborating information: Look at your habits concerning your health problems. Analyze your daily routine. Now research your specific health issues.

Look at your daily schedule. Now research the amount of sleep recommended for an individual of your age. The amount of exercise. Dietary advice. Write down what you have found.

Creating inferences and giving meaning to data: Look at the data you collected in your research. How does it reflect on your assumptions? Does it hint that you should make significant life changes? Does it change how you understand your health and habits?

Write down the main directions in which the data you collected is pointing you. Write down what new important information you have obtained.

Communication and language: Write down what you have learned about your health. Answer the following questions:

1. Is my lifestyle healthy?
2. Am I addressing my health problems?
3. What do I need to do daily to make my life healthier?

Write the answers as clearly as possible. Now read it to a trusted loved one. Ask if they agree with your conclusions and if what you wrote was clear.

Implications and consequences: Now, it is time to develop a plan for a new daily schedule. Take the data you have gathered and your interpretation of it and plan a daily schedule which will:

1. Improve your health over time.
2. Be realistic enough for you to follow.

Now let's look at the process you followed to analyze your health using Bloom's taxonomy. Follow the plan you created for your daily routine for at least a month. Once you have done so, use Bloom's Taxonomy to check your process and to compare the two frameworks to each other:

Remembering: When you started to analyze your health, how did you approach the problem? What were your first thoughts on how to approach the problem?

Understand: Once you had gathered the relevant information and resources, did you put enough of a conscious effort into understanding them? Did you understand them correctly? What information did you misinterpret at this point?

Apply: When you started to develop an action plan, was it based on the knowledge and resources you had gathered previously? Did you ignore any important information? Did you realize you were missing any information?

Analyze: Think of the moment you came up with your initial plan designed to overcome the challenges you faced. How well did you draw on the information you had gathered previously? Were your analysis of the problem and its solution the best you could muster based on the information you had at the time? Or did you make mistakes in analyzing the data you had at your fingertips?

Evaluate: When you tackled the problem, did you have a plan, or did you improvise? Was it well constructed? Was it too optimistic or pessimistic?

Create: Did you put the plan you had constructed into action? Did you focus on some parts more than others? What went wrong? Was it because there was a flaw in your planning, or were obstacles you could not predict?

Now answer the following questions at length:

1. What was the strongest part of your problem-solving process in this case?
2. What was the weakest part of your problem-solving process?
3. Now that you are familiar with the Elder-Paul framework and Bloom's Taxonomy, what would you have done differently?
4. How do the two approaches differ in tackling problems? Which will you use in the future and why?

## Conclusion

We learned from the models presented here that we should use critical thinking as a part of a wider plan whenever possible. A good idea on its own is not enough. The Paul-Elder framework and Bloom's taxonomy provide us with excellent guidelines for utilizing critical thinking in a structured way.

Sometimes we have an inspired idea and want to reveal it to the world. Sony sure did. But they did not plan their steps well. Better market research would have revealed that consumers desire longer tapes and care less about picture quality. That is human.

There are always flaws in any plan, and we cannot predict all important elements in advance. But if we plan correctly, we can minimize the negative impact of surprises. By applying the elements of reasoning, we also learn to think on our feet when we are surprised.

Sony's biggest mistake was its executives' inability to alter their assumptions as new data came in. As it became clear that Betamax was failing, they did not change their strategy and remained fixated on picture quality. They continued that strategy for a good twenty-five years after it was apparent to everyone that the model had failed.

There is no doubt the people working at Sony at the time were very bright. However, they were too entrenched in their approach and too prideful to admit mistakes.

## 3
## THE EVOLUTION OF A CRITICAL MIND: WHAT SETS CRITICAL THINKERS APART

King Solomon would sit in judgment, as kings did in those days, parceling out justice. One day two women came before him and presented Solomon with a complicated case. Both were mothers to newborn babies and shared a single tent.

One night, a horrible tragedy occurred. One of the babies died in their sleep. Now the two mothers claimed the remaining child as their own. Unfortunately, there were no reliable witnesses or useful evidence to consult. Therefore, they asked the great king to determine to whom the living baby belonged.

The king pondered this difficult case before suddenly ordering, "bring me my sword!" The alarmed women asked what the sword was for, and the king replied, "since we do not know who the mother is, we shall cut the baby in half and give each woman an equal share."

One of the women accepted the judgment and said that no one should have the living baby if she couldn't have the living baby. However, the other woman cried out, "Give the baby to her, just don't kill him!" Solomon smiled widely and ruled that the baby belonged to the woman who showed selfless love to the living child.

The judgment is renowned. Many consider it an example of profound wisdom. Why? After all, Solomon had ordered an insane verdict. Splitting the baby would have assured its death.

However, Solomon understood human nature. He knew that one of the women before him was a despondent mother of a recently lost baby, who had so much bitterness within her that she was trying to deprive her friend of her child. Meanwhile, the other woman was a loving mother to a living child.

By suggesting cutting the baby in half, Solomon hoped to bring out the bitterness in one of the women and the selfless love in the other. The test he devised succeeded in doing both and ultimately in solving the problem.

Though some may refer to Solomon's judgment as an example of unbiased judicial wisdom, it is the product of significant emotional intelligence.

In his successful attempt at understanding the two mothers' emotional inner world, the king displayed a key element of critical thinking: empathy.

The ability to be a true and influential critical thinker requires certain personality traits. The deepest critical thinker is not necessarily the smartest person. Rather, critical thinkers tend to be smart, talented individuals with certain personality traits. These include open-mindedness, humility, and empathy [1].

**Portrait Of A Critical Mind**

In this chapter, we will take a deep dive into the characteristics of critical thinking individuals. As you might expect, critical thinkers are analytical and careful thinkers. However, they also possess emotional and ethical gifts, which we do not always associate with reason and thought. A genuine critical thinker exhibits a combination of traits.

Remember that even if you do not possess some of these characteristics (and you certainly do have at least a few of them), you can work on improving these aspects in your thought process. The mind is like a muscle. If you exercise your mind the right way, your critical thinking faculties can improve by leaps and bounds.

In our preconceptions, we imagine capable thinkers as people of great knowledge and intelligence. These are indeed desirable qualities for a critical thinker. However, a critical thinker is not necessarily smarter than a non-critical thinker. Rather they couple their intelligence with systematic thinking and emotional courage. Quite often, it requires the willingness to stand up for unpopular ideas.

Everyone has had that nagging feeling that something about the common wisdom just isn't right. However, it is easier just to get along. Everyone notices that commonly held beliefs can be flawed. Critical thinkers differ in their willingness to explore different options.

Some of the smartest people out there see the world through their particular lens. They treat all information that runs counter to their world-view as a nuisance. These limited but influential thinkers use their intelligence to get what they want.

Here are some of the main characteristics of critical thinkers [2].

**Truth-Seeker**

Critical thought involves the relentless pursuit of the truth. That means gathering data and analyzing it to reveal the true nature of things.

Critical thinkers value honesty from others. But most importantly, they are honest with themselves. People very commonly like to reassure themselves and others with little white lies. But when we are making high-stakes action plans, brutal honesty can save time and money. It is important to remember, a plan based on inaccuracies is highly likely to go awry.

For example, when we work on our plans, we should accept criticism and examine it on its merits. Taking personal offense will prevent us from taking valuable advice into account. In addition, if we discourage the input of others, they will not give it in the future. Again, this will lead to the loss of helpful input.

**Systematic**

A systematic person will actively seek to work through their actions carefully and methodically. This means before they take a complex action, they will design and then execute a detailed and in-depth plan of how they plan to achieve their specified goal.

If you look at Bloom's Taxonomy or the Paul-Elder framework, you will see that they are actively divided into logical parts. Together, those parts were intentionally configured to make up a systematic rubric of critical thinking. When we think critically, we must never skip a step and only move on once every part of our plan has been thoroughly completed.

No matter how good your intuition may be, there is no substitute for seeking out all relevant knowledge.

One example of the active pursuit of systematic thinking by critical thinkers pertains to obtaining background knowledge. They systematically gather all of the relevant information on the topic and analyze it carefully.

Once they have gathered the relevant information, critical thinkers will follow a clear and logical path to resolving the problem at hand.

Our previous reviews of the Elder-Paul framework and Bloom's taxonomy provide us with good examples of following a systematic path towards resolving our problems.

## Analytical

It is easy to get lost in all the details which go into problem-solving. An analytical mind is capable of both locating problems and solving them. A critical thinker will remain focused on the most important components rather than get lost in the details.

For example, an analytical mind can look through all of the data and information gathered to develop a plan and find the biggest obstacles. When predicting the biggest obstacles facing a specific action plan, critical thinkers formulate contingencies and determine how to overcome them.

## Open-Minded

No amount of intelligence can make up for close-mindedness. Most people are more likely to reject information coming from a source they dislike. However, a critical thinker will never dismiss information based only on its source. They will do their best to evaluate its validity on its own merits.

For example, many decision-makers dismiss the ideas of their subordinates at work. The opinion of an individual ranked less senior is less likely to be accepted. However, sometimes individuals with less seniority have fresher ideas and can shake up stale and outdated methods.

Instead of dismissing ideas that we dislike, we should develop the capacity to treat them as fairly as possible.

**Self-Confident**

If critical thinking leads to meaningful action, it must also involve the courage to defend and promote unpopular ideas. Therefore, an influential critical thinker is willing to confidently support true and logical opinions in the face of significant social opposition. This is one of the most challenging and risky elements in wielding critical thinking meaningfully.

A critical thinker must develop the intellectual self-confidence to avoid two potential emotional pitfalls associated with self-doubt. Some people who lack self-confidence are afraid to make plans, thinking they will not be of high quality. Others are unwilling to admit that they may have made a mistake. A critical thinker must avoid both. They must be willing to make their ideas known and accept criticism.

**Inquisitive**

A critical thinker is not lazy. We often parrot the "party line" out of sheer laziness. After all, if we follow the common wisdom, we do not have to analyze our assumptions' logic. To develop new ideas, we must be willing to put in the work to challenge existing orthodoxy. But that is just the start. We need to work even harder to establish alternatives. Many attempts at rethinking our assumptions will lead to dead ends.

At times we fear taking intellectual risks because we may face opposition or embarrassment. However, we need to be willing to make mistakes. There are no shortcuts. Courage and perseverance are essential to the cultivation of critical thinking.

For example, we may find ourselves faced with two plans: one which will bring a worse result but attract less criticism and one which is more efficient but more controversial. Choosing the path of less resistance may seem wise, but it is a betrayal of our commitment to the truth.

## Cognitive And Emotional Mature

The process of honest evaluation of facts involves humility. Critical thinkers realize that new information can and should undermine long-held assumptions. They are brave enough to follow through, despite the mental discomfort and social risk associated with challenging prevailing norms.

It may sound like a paradox, but a critical thinker must develop humility and courage. The two complement each other. It takes courage to admit that you are bad at something or made the wrong decision.

It also takes humility to admit that our emotions can get in the way of accurate analysis. In particular, rage and panic cloud our ability to reason. Putting aside a decision when we are in the wrong emotional frame of mind shows humility. Making a rash decision does not.

For example, parents know they should avoid disciplining their children when angry. Rather they should always be in control of their actions. Punishment should only be applied when it will benefit them.

However, when we are angry, it becomes difficult to discipline our children while taking their long-term benefits into account. When we feel rage, our main driving impulse is to get rid of that feeling. Our rational minds know that if we discipline our children too harshly, it will not benefit their well-being. Therefore, when we apply critical thinking, we catch ourselves before it's too late. We can make similarly bad decisions unless we admit to ourselves: yes, I am angry. No, I should not be making decisions.

A critical thinker is humble enough to confess they are not experts on every issue, nor can they be. You should be willing to listen openly to the ideas of others, even (or especially) if they challenge your conceptions [3].

Charitability: To avoid the "straw man" fallacy, it is important to examine an argument fairly. When presenting arguments we disagree with, we often intentionally portray them as absurd.

When you are trying to be charitable to an argument, you disagree with, execute the following thought exercise. Do not imagine how you will "win" an argument with them. Instead, imagine you need to ask the person making the argument if you understood their viewpoint accurately. What would that person say? Would they think your presentation of their thinking was fair and accurate? Think of the reasons people you disagree with look at the world differently from you. Doing so requires empathy: the ability to put yourself in their shoes.

Humility: We view humility as not a lack of confidence. Instead, it is an honest understanding that our knowledge and comprehension are limited. True humility is the willingness to cheerfully admit that our self-worth does not depend on always being right.

A genuine critical thinker knows they will be wrong about things. Often. They also possess the cognitive maturity to re-examine their assumptions and get it right the second time.

**Foresight**

No one can read the future, but the process of critical thinking can alleviate a great deal of doubt and uncertainty around future developments. After gathering all the relevant data and analyzing it, a critical thinker should make a reasonable estimation of the most likely developments and plan accordingly.

Without at least some foresight, we are unable to plan for the future. Risk analysis is key when solving-problems. A critical thinker will have contingencies worked out for all the most likely eventualities.

We can cultivate foresight by developing an understanding of how others think. In the cut-throat business world, many see empathy as a sign of weakness because of the association with an inability to stand up for themselves.

This is a misunderstanding of the concept. In the context of critical thinking, empathy refers to your ability to understand how others think and why.

The great military strategist Sun Tzu advised, "know your opponent and know yourself, in a hundred battles you will never be in peril." The key to defeating your enemy is to understand their aspirations and hopes. If you know what another person is trying to achieve, it is far easier to prevent them from reaching it.

Do not confuse empathy with sympathy. Sympathy involves identifying with another individual or group to the point that you can feel what they do. A deep sympathy may indeed impinge on your critical thinking by forming an emotional bias. Instead, you should cultivate the ability to *understand* what another is feeling and why.

We have a natural tendency to make negative assumptions about the thought process of others. We often believe that the reasoning behind an argument we disagree with is inferior to our efforts. We assume our rival is ill-informed or does not have all of the facts. A critical thinker has intellectual integrity.

Another common assumption is that others are making their arguments in bad faith. We may find ourselves thinking, perhaps this person is trying to undermine my position at work and therefore disagrees with me.

Next time you listen to a politician you profoundly disagree with, notice how you respond. Do you feel your breath quicken and the beginning of a slight headache? Do you feel a vague angry feeling in the pit of your stomach? You may ask yourself, how could any reasonable person hold these views.

Just listening to these views makes you uncomfortable. You will almost certainly have an urge to change the channel.

Next time you turn on the news, don't change the channel. Instead, do the following exercise. What do you think of the politician espousing these views? Make a list of the traits you associate with this person. Your answer will almost certainly contain slights on their intelligence or good faith. Often you will not think highly of either.

This is your brain protecting its sense of certainty by shutting out different viewpoints.

Intellectual integrity is the ability to treat the arguments of others fairly. Other people may indeed be ill-informed or biased in their analysis. However, if we are honest, our analysis is also not wholly pure.

Our own conscious and unconscious biases play a significant role in shaping our thoughts and opinions. We also have significant gaps in our information and knowledge, just like everyone else. No one we know is an objective fountain of untainted wisdom and expertise.

When we practice true intellectual integrity, we put aside our biases about the other person's intellectual or moral inferiority. Instead, we judge the argument on its own merits.

**Action Steps**

The Supreme Court has hundreds of decisions on controversial and important topics. The judges at this institution use critical thinking to decide the most important issues of the day.

Pick a notable Supreme Court decision on a topic that interests you. The official website includes all Supreme Court decisions from 2014 to the current day:

https://www.supremecourt.gov/opinions/slipopinion/20

The judgments have a series of justices either concurring with or dissenting from the court's final decisions. Analyze the arguments each justice uses following the traits of critical thinkers. Rate each justice from 1-10 on this scale. Try not to let your previous opinions on the issue you have selected influence your rating. You should rely just on the quality of the argument made by each justice.

Make sure to do some research on the case before you read the opinions. For example, read the Wikipedia page on the case and some news reports on it. This is an important exercise because research is a crucial part of critical thinking!

Truth-Seeking: Did the justice seem more interested in promoting a narrow agenda or seeking the genuine and objective truth about the issue?

Open-Minded: How did each justice treat the information which countered their opinion and world view? Were they fair or dismissive? Was there important information mentioned by justices on the opposing side of the decision they neglected to mention? Why do you think that is?

Analytical: How well did each justice analyze the application of the law to the case? How much attention did they give to the implications of the ruling? Did their analysis ring true to you, or did it seem to further a specific agenda?

Systematic: Did they apply the elements of the law and their logical reasoning evenly and using the same system throughout their judgment? Did they look at all the relevant elements or pick and choose to make their point stronger?

Self-confident: Are the justices hesitant or forceful in how they present their views? Is their confidence in the rightfulness of their opinion genuine or just an act? How willing are they to admit that they may be wrong or that some information contradicts their opinions?

Inquisitive: Do a little background checking on the justices and their legal specialties and backgrounds. How willing are they to step out of their comfort zones? How important is it to seek out new information that will shed new light on the case, regardless of their preconceptions?

Cognitively mature: How aware are the justices of the complexity of the situation? Do they avoid the urge to simplify the case to make a ruling easier? How much wisdom and experience is behind their decision and reasoning?

Now, look at yourself. Who did you agree with before you read the opinions? Did reading it change your mind in any way? Why? Most importantly, ask yourself: were you as receptive to opinions you disagreed with as you were to those you agreed with?

Remember, developing critical thinking aims to reach the point where we evaluate all information fairly, regardless of the source. This can be challenging. As you can see, even the Supreme Court justices have trouble with that.

But they should keep trying, and so should you!

## Conclusion

When King Solomon sat in judgment, he did not look down at the two women before him. He put himself in their shoes and asked, "what would I do in that situation?" His cognitive maturity gave him the foresight to predict how the situation would play out.

Critical thinkers do not sit cold and aloof while judging the world. They are connected to their environment and understand it. They actively seek out new information and are not afraid to be challenged. They then use the information and insights they have gained to understand how the world works.

## 4
## BARRIERS TO CRITICAL THINKING

An old air force maxim said, "if you're not catching flak, you're not over the target." Experience taught the pilots that flying over a high-value target attracts enemy fire. With the limited means of target identification available at the time, the anti-aircraft fire intensity was a good indicator that the pilot was on the right track.

There was another element to this as well. It was considered manly to tough and bomb through enemy fire. The worst thing a bomber crew could do was avoid a tough target and try to dump the bombs elsewhere. Nothing could harm your reputation as an airman more than that.

On August 1, 1943, 177 allied bombers took off from Benghazi in Libya. Their mission was to bomb Nazi operated oil refineries in Romania. One of the formations involved was the 376th Bombardment Group of the United States Air Force.

The Group took a wrong turn and ended up over Bucharest, the capital of Romania. As they approached the city, they faced enemy flak fire. However, Commander Keith Compton saw conspicuously civilian looking buildings below him. He had to make a snap decision. Remembering the maxim, he decided to order the payloads dropped.

Just then, another squadron broke radio silence and warned of the mistake. Had they failed to intervene, they could have been responsible for the deaths of countless innocent lives. Commander Compton almost made a terrible mistake due to his preconceived beliefs.

The brave Commander almost fell victim to a common barrier to critical thinking: a prior unexamined belief.

As we will see in this chapter, beliefs, biases, intuition and certain emotions can be a barrier to critical thinking. However, with self-awareness, we can overcome these obstacles. Pay careful attention here, so you know what to avoid!

**Beliefs**

The costly mistake Commander Compton nearly made is an example of affirming the consequent. This logical fallacy occurs in two stages. First, a person believes that an outcome is likely to occur under specific circumstances. Second, when that outcome materializes, the same person assumes those preconceived circumstances were the cause of it [1].

However, this is often a fallacy. A completely separate explanation may cause the outcome. The circumstances that led to the outcome in one instance may not apply in another.

In its most primitive form, the fallacy of affirming the consequent looks like this: Paris is in Europe. Therefore, if I am in Europe, I am in Paris. Fallacies this extreme are quite rare [2].

Why do we make such costly mistakes? In a complex environment, we are unable to process all relevant information in real-time. Hence, we rely on simplifications to make quick decisions. In so doing, we rely heavily on unexamined beliefs we have accepted earlier in life [3].

This tendency is completely human. However, when stakes are high, we cannot accept preconceived cultural assumptions. In these cases, identifying and examining our ingrained assumptions can be the difference between life and death.

Critical thinkers show a willingness to examine ingrained ideals thoroughly and objectively. Therefore, the ability to question even our most cherished cultural ideals is at the heart of critical thinking. It is uncomfortable to think that the ideas we take for granted are dulling our thinking. But that does not mean it isn't true.

This does not mean that we necessarily abandon the cultural notions and traditions we are comfortable with. Instead, we will now have the courage to see how they stand up to rational criticism. We may come out of the process with renewed confidence in our beliefs because they have stood the test.

In other cases, new evidence may change our minds. Another option is to conclude that we maintain our faith or certain ideas for cultural reasons rather than rational ones. That is fine, as long as we are aware of it and consider that when making decisions. The point is to be open to any outcome which is supported by the evidence.

Whatever the result is, applying critical analysis is beneficial to the depth of our faith. After examining our principles, we will enjoy renewed confidence that our beliefs represent the truth as we understand it.

Consider what your cultural beliefs are. What did you get from your parents, school, workplace? Are there assumptions behind them? Do they make sense? Have you ever started to question them before but then stopped yourself? Have these beliefs and assumptions ever held you back from achieving your potential?

Reexamining your deepest held beliefs can be a painful process. However, if you are honest with yourself, figuring this out will make a world of difference. Your rational decision-making process will improve greatly as a result.

**Biases**

A bias is when an individual has either a strong preference or aversion to something, regardless of its merits. It is an unfair way of looking at the world, but one which we all practice often.

We do not generate or accept ideas to satisfy intellectual curiosity. We do so to satisfy our emotional needs. Studies show that our brain would do anything to avoid the suffering that accompanies doubt. Therefore, our brain actively seeks out ideas that will bring order and certainty into our lives.

We develop our thought patterns as a means of dealing with uncertainty. Anytime we are confronted with an unprecedented situation, we may experience anxiety and stress. Therefore, from childhood and onward, our mind constantly seeks out certainty.

We think of our early years as a time of great joy. However, anxiety is an integral part of our formative years. After all, it is a stage where so much of what children encounter is unprecedented and frightening.

A young child is hungry for trusted sources of information to alleviate their anxiety. Thus, children hungrily consume input from parents and teachers. Information from these sources enjoys priority since it comes from a position of authority. Therefore, we base our understanding of how the world works on our experiences in that formative period.

Our mind develops a habit of seeking out certainty instead of truth. This follows us into adulthood: we cling to trusted but unexamined information and values. We remain hesitant to give up these answers, as that would increase the level of uncertainty in our lives [4]. Therefore, we often follow a truth-seeking critical thought process. Although clinging to our biases can be reassuring, it clouds our judgment and makes it more likely that we will make costly mistakes.

**Intuition**

Intuition is an attempt to gain knowledge without in-depth reasoning. It has often been regarded as a flawed manner of thinking by philosophers. However, psychological and cognitive studies of human thought patterns have revealed that this is the default manner in which our brain functions.

Usually, when we decide, we combine limited elements of reasonable thought with a significant amount of intuition. This thinking mode allows for successful short-term goals without using the full energy required to process critical thought.

Heuristics are how we turn our intuition into thoughts and action plans. Research shows that the vast majority of our estimations and solutions to problems are based on them [5].

Let's see how these work in a real-life situation. Very often, we will employ a "trial and error" approach.

Imagine you have little experience with wine but find yourself spending time in France. Everyone seems to order wine at dinner, and you don't want to feel left out. You look at the menu and recognize the names. That doesn't help you much. However, you are too self-conscious to ask your hosts what to order. What do you do when the waiter asks for the order?

Maybe you will order a cabernet because you like the name. It is quite possible that you love it and order it next time, thereby solving your wine order problem. At least for now. Maybe you hate it, and next time you will try a merlot. You had absolutely no idea if cabernet was the right choice, but you were willing to make a mistake and try to do better next time. This form of heuristic is called "trial and error."

Perhaps rather than go into your wine ordering adventure blind, you try to remember if you know anything at all about wine. You recall you heard somewhere that red wine pairs well with meat, while white works with seafood. Having ordered Chateaubriand, you order a random red wine. This has a better chance of success than the "trial and error" method since this rule is generally accurate.

Using this type of heuristic known as a "rule of thumb," you at least can avoid ordering a wine that tastes disgusting with your food. However, that does not mean you will like the wine.

A critical thinking approach to ordering the best wine would, in theory, provide us with better results. It would involve researching which wine goes best with a specific dish. What vintages are on offer? What is on the menu? Does the offer price represent good value for money? Does the refrigerator properly chill white wine? And many other factors.

Would following this process be worth it for ordering wine? Almost definitely not. The stakes are low. At worst, we drink wine we don't like or get silently judged by our hosts. To many people being adventurous is fun. We have limited time and brainpower to spend on every decision, and heuristics are usually good enough. Also, imagine what the people around you would think if they knew you were taking wine selection that seriously. There are social costs to the critical thinking process.

But it's more than that. As long as we believe in them, quick answers—whether correct or not—immediately alleviate the pain caused by uncertainty. The long and uncertain process of questioning our assumptions is counterintuitive, as it does not provide quick answers. Worse, it may result in questioning long-held beliefs that have protected us from uncertainty for years. By exposing us to the real uncertainty around us, critical thinking can increase anxiety in the short term. This is why heuristics make up the vast majority of our decisions. This is not a bad thing in all instances.

However, heuristics may work too well but not to our advantage. We get used to expending little effort into making decisions, even when they are crucially important. But simplified thinking of this sort leads to all kinds of fallacies. One form of this is the composition fallacy. This occurs when we attribute one member of the group's characteristics to encompass every individual associated with that group.

Let's look at how this works and imagine the following example: at a party, we meet a person from two towns over. This individual spends the entire party being obnoxious and rude to everyone. Since we have never been to that town, our main association with it is now unpleasant. However, when we visit that beautiful town, we meet countless lovely people. This is a reminder that we should not be quick to generalize.

A similar common example of illogical thinking is the association fallacy. When we fall victim to this fallacy, we consider a blameless individual to be "guilty by association." This is when we consider someone who has ties to a wrongdoer to be guilty, through no fault of their own.

Another fallacy is the ad hominem attack. In this fallacy, we focus on discrediting the source of the argument rather than its validity. When we practice an ad-hominem attack, we find reasons to doubt the source based on information that is unrelated to the argument we are engaged with.

Once we have discredited the source of the argument by attacking it on irrelevant grounds, we may feel that we have rendered their argument invalid. But we have not. No source is perfect and even the most discredited source is capable of making strong arguments on occasion. We must rise above the temptation of focusing on the source, and instead train our faculties on the argument.

In conclusion, heuristics are mental shortcuts. They are useful in certain circumstances. If we are engaged in low stakes decisions, such as where to have dinner tonight or which brand of instant coffee to purchase, heuristics are a perfectly acceptable way to make the decision. We do not always have the time or the energy to employ the full process of critical thinking.

However, when an important problem arises at work or in your private life, avoid the temptation of relying on heuristics. Instead, begin the systematic and active application of critical thinking to the problem. When dealing with important issues, you should never settle for anything less.

**Emotions**

We tend to think of critical thinking as a rational exercise, one which can only be hindered by our emotions. This is only partially accurate.

It is true that in some instances, our emotions can be a hindrance to critical thinking. As discussed previously, this mostly relates to what we think of as negative emotions. Anger is incompatible with critical thought. When we are angry, we tend to lash out to relieve ourselves from uncomfortable emotions.

The trouble is that we do not weigh the consequences of our actions. When we act out of anger, we end up in a worse situation than before.

But some emotions make us think more carefully and apply more effort to analysis and solutions. For example, if we have a passion for a subject or care deeply about a goal, that energy can be channeled into critical thinking. Just make sure to take a deep breath before beginning the process of working on an issue you care about deeply. Make sure to follow a reliable process such as those presented in the Paul-Elder framework and the Bloom taxonomy. Let your passion feed your interest but do not allow it to dictate your process.

Emotions can also help us frame our problems morally and usefully. For example, the United Nations founded the World Food Program to fight world hunger. The compassion many well-meaning people felt for the malnourished around the world generated the interest and effort necessary to get the program off the ground.

The World Food Program actively and decisively utilized critical thinking to launch this effort and render it effective. Having a limited budget, the United Nations needed to find cheap and reliable sources of food and to reach out and locate the hungriest and neediest individuals.

The logistical planning eagerly pursued in order to reach some of the most devastated parts of the world is mind-boggling. As a result of these persistent efforts, the organization has fed 97 million people in 88 countries. It aims to reduce world hunger to zero by 2030 [6].

The effect of emotions on critical thinking is complex. The right emotions can bring out our best problem-solving instincts. In all honesty, emotions can cloud our judgment and hinder our reasoning process. However, positive emotions can help us frame our critical thinking process by reminding us of what is important: making the world a better place. Meanwhile, negative emotions usually cloud our judgment and make us pursue the wrong objectives, such as satiating our insecurities or our need for revenge.

The good news is that it is easy to differentiate between positive and negative emotional influences. All of those emotions that many people actively consider negative are hindrances. Anger, jealousy, self-righteousness, and pride are obstacles to critical thought. Empathy, compassion, and generosity help us think and make us think of others instead of ourselves.

On the other hand, some emotions get in the way and muddle our thinking. Have you ever tried to make an important decision when you were angry? How did that work out for you? Similarly, we do not want to dismiss ideas and evidence because we dislike the source. Selfishness and jealousy can constrain us from doing what is good for the people around us.

There are two good rules of thumb here.

First rule: if your emotions are going to be involved in the process (and they very often should be), make sure they are your noble emotions. Empathy, patience, and tolerance are incredible emotions and very helpful in engendering critical thought. Anger, pettiness, and jealousy are undesirable at the best of times and only hinder rational thought.

Second rule: Emotions (only the good ones!) can be essential in defining problems and setting out their solutions. They are far less useful in determining the process you follow once the goals and issues are determined. For example, do not allow emotions to determine how you weigh the evidence and which data to take seriously.

We can't and shouldn't stop feeling. It is what makes us human, and our best emotions make life worth living. Just remember to let the bad ones pass before you start reasoning.

**Action Steps**

We will now take some steps to examine the role that these obstacles have played in your decision-making so far. By doing so, we can craft the past path towards future improvement.

Think of three important decisions you have made in the following three fields: your love life, career, and finances.

Write down your answers honestly:

Bias:

1. Did you examine all of the options available to you, or did you dismiss options without further examination?
2. Did you dismiss viable options due to bias, or were they all dismissed for rational reasons?
3. If bias played a role, what was your bias?
4. Did your bias have negative or positive consequences?
5. How will you overcome this bias and similar bias in future decisions?

Intuition:

1. When you made your decision, was it primarily rational or intuitive?
2. What was your intuition telling you?
3. Has relying on your intuition had negative or positive consequences?
4. Was the decision too important to be made based on intuition?
5. How will you figure out in the future whether a decision is also important for an intuition-based approach?

Beliefs:

1. Make a list of beliefs you consider important to

your identity and not shared by everyone around you.
2. Look at each belief; did they influence any of the three decisions?
3. Was the influence of your beliefs positive or negative?
4. Were you aware of the influence of your beliefs on your decision-making at the time?
5. How will you remain aware of the influence of your beliefs on decisions you make in the future?

Emotions:

1. What emotions influenced your decision-making process?
2. Which would you qualify as useful and which do you believe served as hindrances?
3. How did your emotions influence the outcome?
4. What did your positive emotions (such as empathy) do in terms of influencing the process?
5. What influence did your negative emotions (such as anger) have on your critical thought?

Write down your answers. Next time you have an important decision to make, consult these questions and your answers before deciding. When you have concluded writing down your answers, make sure to go over those answers yet again.

How did your awareness of these barriers influence your decision-making? Remember, we all face barriers and obstacles to critical thinking. However, when we are aware of them, we take away most of their power.

**Conclusion**

When we face a problem, resolving it through critical thinking is not our first instinct. We prefer to spend less time resolving the problem, avoiding questioning our beliefs, and trusting our intuition. The truth is, for most decisions we make in our lives, this process is good enough. We do not need to employ Bloom's Taxonomy from start to finish to put in our lunch order.

We should employ the time-consuming process of critical thinking for the important decisions in life and our most complicated career-related problems. We can't use it for every small decision, nor should we. But when it comes to those decisions, we must avoid relying primarily on intuition, beliefs, and biases. As Captain Compton discovered, it can be a matter of life or death.

## 5
## READY, SET, GO: APPLYING CRITICAL THINKING TO YOUR PERSONAL AND PROFESSIONAL LIFE

We have looked at how critical thought works in theory. But what about in practice? How do we apply these principles in our daily lives? No matter the setting we are in, life throws us some unexpected obstacles.

What happens when we put our best ideas to the test of reality? What if things don't go to plan? When our critical thinking process comes off the page, we find we have to deal with real people. They react in unpredictable ways that can confound our best-laid plans.

Think of the plight of Coca Cola during the "Coke Wars" with Pepsi. Their sales had gone down in the early 1980s, due to the success of their rivals. In response, they changed the product. Renaming their top-selling drink "New Coke" and sweetened it to appeal to the growing teenage market.

It did not work. The loyal Coca Cola customers were outraged. Tens of thousands of calls and letters complaining about the new taste flooded headquarters in Atlanta. To add insult to injury, teenagers continued to prefer Pepsi.

Coca Cola had lost its old customers and failed to gain new ones. An organization called the Old Cola Drinkers of America popped out and received hundreds of thousands of dollars in contributions.

Coca Cola marketing executives soon realized that the original recipe had never been the problem. It remained beloved throughout the country. Instead, sales had been flagging due to poor marketing. There had been no need for the new formula to begin with.

A mere 79 days after introducing the new formula, the company reinstated the old recipe, having renamed it Coca Cola Classic. The Coke executives gave the founder of Old Cola Drinkers of America the first big case of the new-old drink. The response to the return of the old taste was so enthusiastic that one executive commented wryly, "You would have thought we'd cured cancer."

To capture the teenage market, the company launched a new campaign. It featured a bizarre pixelated computer figure in suit and tie, known as Max Headroom, who would alternate comments with computer modulated sound effects. This worked spectacularly and increased sales in that demographic. From then on, the company launched successful campaigns targeted at teenagers.

Meanwhile, the company did not waver from its tried and true formula.

We learn from this that it is not enough to have a good theoretical plan based. We need to tailor it to the real world. We need to be realistic and understand how to put our ideas into practice and convince others to help us.

This chapter will look at methods for applying critical thinking principles to different areas of our lives. We have to adjust our plans to the lay of the land. Don't make the same mistake Coca Cola made. Look at your specific environment and the people around you, and make plans that will stand the test of reality.

**Applying Critical Thinking**

Now you are ready to produce results. This is where the rubber meets the road, and developments come at you fast and furious. But that doesn't mean you can afford to stop reasoning.

After reading the previous chapters, we should understand the fundamentals of critical thought. We should have some idea of what a logical and illogical argument looks like.

Having looked at Bloom's Taxonomy and the Paul-Elder framework, we know how to solve problems and make better decisions. We should apply this knowledge to all facets of our lives. Our family life, careers, education, friendships, and romantic lives can benefit from clear and logical thinking.

In this chapter, we will look at how the unpredictability of life can threaten our best-laid plans. But remember, with some foresight and reasonable responses, the confident critical thinker can respond well to any crisis.

As you put the plan into action, you will run into some inevitable surprises. Treat these surprises not as setbacks but rather as the introduction of new relevant data.

When things do not go according to plan, do not react immediately. This is how we make mistakes. Take a walk outside. Meditate if you are into that. Then go back to the planning stage. What does the new data mean for the validity of your plan? Adjust it accordingly. Think of your plan as a living-breathing organism rather than a completed work set in stone.

**Critical Thinking In Real Life Situations**

Critical thinking is the ability to think through connected ideas thoroughly and independently based solely on reason and evidence. It is the focused and disciplined act of turning our mental abilities towards the resolution of real-world problems.

As one would expect, the people who practice critical thinking are intelligent and knowledgeable. They are also systematic and analytical in their problem-solving approach. They are also cognitively mature and empathetic. Above all, they seek the truth.

Critical thinkers are open-minded and inquisitive and do not allow bias to affect the objective analysis. On the emotional side, they are self-confident and cognitively mature enough to understand their own emotions and others' emotions. The process of critical thought provides those who wield it with a great deal of foresight into real-life developments.

When we use these tools, we become critical thinkers ourselves. As a result, we become more adept at detecting illogical reasoning and fallacies in our thoughts and in the ideas put forth by others. We are now less likely to make bad arguments or rely on untrustworthy data. Finally, we become better decision-makers. Perhaps most importantly, we can make the world around us better by solving consequential problems.

But this is all theoretical. How do we utilize our critical thinking skills in real-life situations? Here is a non-exhaustive list of examples.

**The Internet**

Gathering data and information is a crucial element of critical thinking. This can be trickier than it sounds.

In our ideal models of critical thinking, we gather trustworthy information and process it objectively. However, in reality, how do we know which information is accurate, and what is misleading? Unreliable sources of information sometimes dupe even experts. What chance does the majority of casual researchers have?

When we think of doing research, we shouldn't necessarily imagine the kind of impressive library you find in an Ivy League school or Harry Potter. The simple truth is, most research today is conducted on Google. When asked how they do research, less than 2% of undergraduate students mentioned non-internet sources.

In today's world, we rely on the internet for an increasingly large amount of information. Just Googling a topic will provide you with a great deal of information, some written by well-known professors and others by internet trolls. Unfortunately, a great deal of what we will find is not information. It is disinformation.

How can we tell the difference? Here are some useful benchmarks.

**Who Is The Website Attributed To?**

<u>Not attributed or attributed to someone without known credentials</u>: If you do not know who wrote the entry you are reading or what they know about the topic, be cautious. The individual could be highly reliable, completely ignorant, or have a very strong bias in one direction or another.

<u>Attributed to an interested party</u>: Individuals or organizations with strong credentials potentially provided

this information. However, they may strongly invest in a particular point of view. Even if the source you are using is recognizable or respected, examine their reputation for bias before relying on the information.

These caveats apply to government sources, popular media, think tanks, and highly informed blogs. Use these sources but with caution. They are often more useful in telling us what the prevailing opinions are rather than providing factual information.

Scientific Sources: No source is perfect, but those run by universities and scientific foundations are more reliable than most. Journal articles must go through peer-review to be published. This means other experts and scientists critically examine the source's claims and find any problems or inaccuracies in it. It is best to always use these sources, particularly if you are working on an important project.

An important rule of thumb with any information source, particularly with the internet, is to cross sources. If you want to make sure your information is reliable, make sure it appears in more than one reliable source [1].

**Classroom**

Researchers have tied the development of critical thinking to educational development. For generations, students memorized answers, poems, and the multiplication table and got good grades.

Tests were standardized, and teachers taught students by rote. This made teachers, assessors, and students' lives relatively easy because no one had to overthink. However, that was also the problem.

This approach encouraged young minds to acquire and maintain knowledge. However, it did not encourage them to think. But during the Twentieth Century, it had become increasingly clear that traditional teaching methods did not prepare students for real life.

As America moved to an information and services-based economy, workers had to deal with unpredictable problems daily. Just as importantly, as citizens in a democracy, they would need to analyze information critically to elect or be elected for office.

By the end of the Century, teachers agreed that one of their major responsibilities was to encourage critical thinking. Just about every curriculum published these days mentions the encouragement of critical thinking as a primary objective.

Yet this does not seem to have made a great deal of difference in the capabilities of students. Why is teaching critical thinking so difficult? Is it possible to teach and learn these skills?

The answer is a resounding yes. The truth is, no one needs to learn critical thinking. We are inquisitive creatures by nature. Think of all the inventions human beings have created and all the obstacles they have overcome to bring the science and technology we depend on into the world. Each breakthrough represents the human instinct for solving problems by applying critical thinking.

But our minds can be lazy. Plato, one of Socrates' students, once wrote, "a need or problem encourages creative efforts to meet the need or solve the problem." We usually shorten this to "necessity is the mother of invention." When circumstances thrust us into insecurity there is no end to human ingenuity and inventiveness. Our capacity for cognitive laziness when we are unmotivated is similarly limitless.

The focus in teaching or learning critical thinking should not be on teaching the fundamentals of problem-solving. After all, reciting Bloom's Taxonomy by rote is just more memorization.

Students need to be encouraged to use their existing critical learning faculties.

Methods of encouraging critical thinking in the classroom:

1) Project-based learning: The best way to engage students in critical thinking is by giving them projects to work on. We should not design these projects with a single solution in mind. Rather they should be open-ended so that students may deal with unpredictable problems as they arise. Projects motivate students because they develop a sense of ownership over the result.

2) <u>Question Generation</u>: Encourage students to ask their questions on the topic. One of the most important elements in developing critical thinking skills is learning to question. Yet, we usually are provided with questions to answer.

Asking the students to come up with the questions themselves has two advantages. It helps them develop a knack for questioning. By coming up with their approaches, students also focus on the elements they are interested in and feel more engaged. This encourages natural curiosity.

Studies show that the ability to generate your questions requires a higher level of understanding than answering questions or summarizing material.

A highly successful in the class game uses the model of Jeopardy! Gameshow. Once students have studied a topic, they can construct a table of questions in this format, which, as we all know, divides questions into categories and orders them according to levels of difficulty [2].

**Workplace**

There was a time when a person was hired to a specific job and could expect to work in the same company doing more or less the same thing for their entire careers. Today, the economy is far more dynamic. Therefore, we change jobs far more often, and the work we have often does not fit neatly into our job descriptions.

This means we have to think on our feet to prepare for unexpected challenges at work. This means a workforce with increased critical thinking capacity will likely perform better in the contemporary economy.

Though some individuals work alone and enjoy greater independence in applying critical thinking, most companies and industries require a good deal of teamwork. Therefore, developing critical thinking in the workplace is a team sport.

If so, how do we encourage critical thinking in our working unit?

1) <u>Hire individuals with a predilection for critical thinking</u>: The most obvious way to encourage this approach is by hiring individuals who practice critical thought in their work and respect reasoned thought in others' work. Therefore, you may wish to include open-ended problems in the hiring process.

This will help you weed out workers without critical thinking skills.

2) <u>Encourage a culture of critical thought</u>: You may already have a great deal of unexploited potential for critical thinking at your workplace. However, if individuals are encouraged to stay in their lane and do their job according to the narrowest parameters, it will not come to the fore.

Rigid hierarchy is the enemy of a free-thinking environment. When there is too much regard for hierarchy, workers will follow whatever their superiors say. We call this unhealthy phenomenon "groupthink" [3].

When you have the wrong kind of working environment, employees do not feel safe accepting criticism or criticizing each other. Without trust, individuals can get defensive and suspect malicious intent.

One of the best ways to deal with this problem is to create a "safe zone" meeting. Everyone in the group can criticize others regardless of their rank or personal relationship. The onus is on the superiors, in particular, to encourage those below them to feel comfortable to point out mistakes and differences of opinion.

After completing a project, organize a "lessons learned" meeting to analyze mistakes made and highlight opportunities for future improvement.

3) <u>Stress the process of problem-solving rather than just the solution</u>: Our superiors judge our work performance based on our ability to solve problems quickly and efficiently. Therefore, it is natural that when we confront a professional problem, our first instinct is to prove we can solve it immediately. This often comes at the expense of a full understanding of the implications of the problem. It also encourages "quick fix" solutions rather than creative or in-depth ones.

Rather than jump to a solution, have the team follow the process of critical thinking oriented problem-solving. One of the best ways is to allow the work team to appreciate the problem and its aspects fully. A thorough gathering of data should follow this.

A solution designed after the execution of these preliminary steps will likely be better thought out.

These tips for the promotion of critical thinking in the workplace are top-down ones. But what do you do if you are trying to incorporate critical thinking skills into your work but are having a hard time getting others on board?

Once we have formulated incisive and well-constructed thoughts and arguments, we need to convey them to others. This is a related but very different art form. Unfortunately, it is often the most fallacy ridden type of appeal which is most convincing to audiences. There has always been tension between rhetoric and philosophy. The former focuses on winning over a crowd regardless of the truth. The latter is the art of finding the truth, whether it is convincing or not.

How do we sell our argument?

1) <u>Know your audience</u>: To achieve the result you want, who do you need to convince? What sort of arguments work on that individual?

People tend to think of critical thinking skills as very rational and logical. However, what if the person you need to convince does not respond well to that? If your target is more emotional, take that into account. Some target audiences may be very committed to traditional ways of getting things done. In that case, an argument attacking the "old ways" may be a bad idea.

Appealing to an audience does not mean you alter the essence of your argument. You have reached a superior-conclusion through a process of critical thinking. If altering your argument will bring about inferior results, do not do it. Instead, market your superior product to the proper audience.

2) <u>Clarity</u>: Your argument will not convince even the most receptive crowd if what you are saying is not understood. If your target audience is hostile, they will pounce on any vague elements.

Before conveying your argument to anyone else, make sure it is clear in your head. Some of your terms and the connections between them may appear vague to you or others. Run your argument by a trusted third-party before engaging with the target audience.

Ask them to repeat your argument to you. If they did not understand a key element, the chances are that your audience won't either. Concentrate critical thinking skills like a laser on those weak aspects. Redefine or restructure your argument as needed until it is clear in your mind.

3) <u>Anticipate counterarguments</u>: Even when dealing with a friendly and receptive audience, you may face some backlash or probing questions. Anticipation is doubly important when facing indifferent or hostile listeners. When others express their objections or reservations, make sure you have an answer ready.

You must do this in two stages. First, build a strong alternative to the counterarguments in your initial presentation of the argument. Try to neutralize objections in your initial presentation. Do so by addressing and then neutering likely criticisms. This may not always work. Therefore, have answers prepared for direct challenges to your ideas.

Do not create a strawman of the other person's counterarguments. Remember, your goal is not to convince a bystander who is right. You wish to convince the audience you are addressing that you have the correct answer. It is always tempting to present the rival argument as weaker than it is. Our instinct is to make the other side appear as unconvincing as possible, and sometimes as completely ridiculous, to help us "win."

In attempting to convince others through critical thinking, this is a losing strategy. In terms of the standards of critical thought, this is a form of cheating. When making a "straw man" argument, we are not evaluating which position is the strongest. Instead, we are engaged in a competition of "spin."

At the core of the critical thought is a commitment to a genuine effort to find the best solution to a problem. By genuinely listening to and understanding counterarguments, we may discover flaws in our reasoning. Though this can be an unpleasant experience, it ultimately leads to better outcomes in thought and deed. By being unfair to counterarguments, we are discounting our commitment to truth to build up our ego or reputation.

Aside from the moral argument, there is also a practical win against building a "strawman." When you intentionally misrepresent the arguments of others, they will notice. This may change your target audience's focus from working with you towards a common goal of working against you. Your main goal in facing counter-arguments from your target audience is to assuage their concerns. Keep in mind: the goal is to convince them to join you in realizing your idea. It is not to defeat and humiliate your target audience.

**Home**

We tend to think of home as an arena for warm emotions rather than cold critical thinking. But as we have already discussed, critical thinking can be emotionally motivated and must involve emotional intelligence. Therefore, we can and should use our intellectual abilities to promote our healthy emotional needs and desires.

As we have learned, critical thinking facilitates superior problem solving and is an essential tool for high-stakes problem-solving. Some of the most important problems you will ever face are domestic ones. For example:

- Which home should I buy?
- What college should I send my children to?

- Should I send my elderly parents to a retirement community or care for them myself?
- Should I quit my well-paying job because I am unhappy?
- Should I divorce my spouse?

These may be some of the most high-stakes decisions you will ever make. However, we may suffer the most bias in making decisions related to our family. Yet, we often make these decisions in a disorganized way.

This means critical thinking is an indispensable tool for decision-making at home.

We can also benefit from critical thinking in smaller decisions, such as where to go on holiday and whether to renovate the home.

Finally, if you have children, you have the opportunity to instill the habit of critical thinking into them from an early age.

If so, there are very good reasons to instill an atmosphere of critical thinking at home. Here are some tips on how to do so:

Adopt Transparency: Children often ask their parents why they have to do something. Sometimes our spouse will ask the same thing. Very often, our instinct is to say, "because I said so!" However, studies show that children respond far better intellectually when we clearly explain the rationale behind our actions. This helps them understand that action and thoughts occur within a process and context.

There is another benefit to explaining why we organized things as we have. It forces us to question our logic. Sometimes, we get mad when challenged on our methods because we do things out of habit and rigidity. All of this leads to resentment, confusion, and suboptimal methods.

**Chores**

Explain to everyone why you have arranged the chores and other procedures in the current manner. Listen patiently if anyone, including the children, has comments for improvement and adopt those worthwhile.

Once everyone has agreed, do the following:

1. Explain to everyone clearly what their chores are and why they have to do them.
2. Give the children step-by-step instructions on how to do their chores.
3. Allow the children some choice in what chores they prefer.

When everyone in the family understands the division of chores, everyone operates together to make the home more efficient and comfortable.

**Family Vacation Planning**

Let's face it, when we have children, we often have to make some serious compromises when it is time to take a vacation. When they are very young, they will want to go to Disneyworld and later on they may not want to come with us at all.

There is no way to make everyone happy, but these decisions can create an educational opportunity to impart critical thinking skills to our children. We can also improve our skills in the process.

1) Discuss the possible length of the vacation and the budget to everyone in the family old enough to decide.

2) Ask everyone to come up with their top-three vacation destinations, as long as they are within budget. Every suggestion must come with a list of pros and cons. Agree that there will be a fair vote on the options. One suggestion by each member will advance to the final round.

3) Have each family member make a presentation to convince the others why their suggestion for a family vacation is the best. Then vote on the final destination.

4) Have a family session on what to pack. Everyone in the family can suggest what to bring in order. Then decide who will pack what and carry what.

5) Decide upon activities together in a similar manner to that suggested in step two. Every person in the family

should enjoy at least one activity they are highly interested in. Allow everyone in the family a say while maintaining your final word. If you do so, everyone in the family will feel like they are part of the decision. They will also feel like they are part of the decision-making process. The process will help the kids understand how to make collaborative decisions and what considerations are taken into account when engaging in critical thinking. It will also keep you and your spouse accountable and guarantee you are making decisions for the right reasons.

**Action Steps**

Above you found concrete action steps for integrating critical thinking into your day-to-day life. However, these examples do not cover all of the important areas of your life.

Look at the examples above, and see if you can come up with action steps of your own for the important parts of your life which were not covered here.

Think of coming up with exercises to improve the following elements of your life:

- Your love life
- Your cooking skills
- Your hobbies
- Important friendships
- Maintaining relations with relatives outside your nuclear family

Write them down and engage in them. You can also share them with others also involved in those activities and get their feedback.

If there is one lesson you can get from this chapter, you can apply critical thinking to any important elements in your life. You won't regret it!

**Conclusion**

In this chapter, we learned that after we have made our beautiful, critically-thought-out plans, we have to bring them to fruition in the real world. Whether at work, home, in the classroom, or online, we will run into obstacles. People will stand in our way. Our sources may turn out to be unreliable, we may have to convince skeptical people, and we may face unpleasant surprises along the way.

However, if we have done our homework and have produced a genuinely solid plan based on critical thinking, we should be ok. When you run into obstacles, don't panic. Don't do what Coca Cola did and ditch your product at the first sign of trouble. Dust yourself off and adapt your plan to the circumstances.

## 6

## SIMPLE AND FUN MENTAL EXERCISES TO DEVELOP AND PRACTICE CRITICAL THINKING

We have discussed how to think critically. But how do we bring these skills to bear in our everyday life? English author Malcolm Gladwell famously wrote that to achieve greatness in any endeavor, we must reach 10,000 hours of "deliberate practice." But don't worry, there is no need to spend endless hours on boring exercises. After all, we are not aiming for greatness. Yet! Instead, we are aiming for competence.

Is it even possible to spend a considerable amount of time on critical thinking practice while maintaining our busy schedules? Absolutely. We do so by integrating the practice into our daily lives.

We are already halfway there. Acquiring the habit of thinking critically does not require reinventing yourself. It simply means reinforcing the best tendencies your mind already exhibits. It also involves diminishing the influence of our lazy and destructive thinking habits.

Life provides us with endless dilemmas and problems daily. Every weekday morning, we may face the dilemma, should I buy a coffee, and if so, which one. More consequential decisions also arise on a fairly regular basis. For example, should I ask my boss for a raise? Life provides us with the exercises we need regularly.

We are already exercising critical thinking in resolving these problems. We always at least briefly consider our options and the advantages and disadvantages of different decisions.

## Ill-Defined Problems

What we don't do right now is think the possibilities through systematically. A proven method of developing critical thinking skills is by working through problems with no clear solution.

There are great advantages to working through problems of this sort. Life constantly provides us with ill-defined problems to work through. What is often missing is the inclination to treat day-to-day problems as opportunities to exercise critical thinking.

When we use critical thinking for our everyday problems, we accomplish two amazing things at once. Our brains become sharper and more critical. But more importantly, we make better decisions.

Not all of our decisions will be the right ones. No matter how hard we try, we may be missing crucial information necessary to make the right decision. Or sometimes you make the best decision possible under certain conditions and suffer bad luck. However, the proportion of correct decisions you make will increase. This means your quality of life will improve over time.

Research has shown that critical thinking exercises and games are a useful way of getting in the habit of using our brains differently. The exercises suggested here are a good starting point because they seek to deepen inquiry to connect with our habits and interests. Hopefully, these can help facilitate the incorporation of critical thinking into your daily lives.

**Examples Of An Open-Ended Exercise**

Travel Report

Are you traveling to another part of the country or the world? Is your business expanding into another area? Or, perhaps you are just interested in a specific part of the world? Let's use that relevance or interest to learn about that part of the world.

1) Generate a question about this part of the world that has always interested you. It could relate to the cuisine, politics, culture, arts, or any other feature. Make sure it is a question that cannot be answered by a simple yes or no.

*Example*: Say you are traveling to China. Have you ever wondered what the differences are between the Chinese food you get at a restaurant in the United States and what people eat in China? You may wonder: what are the major regional cuisines in the country?

2) Gather materials to answer your question. Make sure to consult reliable information that is relevant to the question you asked. Try to see if you can cross information on more than one reliable source to make sure that it is true.

*Example*: Use internet sources. Take a book on Chinese food out of the library. Watch a couple of documentaries. See if they are in general agreement about what the major regional cuisines are. See what the main dishes are within each regional cuisine.

3) Analyze the data. Do the sources you have disagree? What are the disagreements? Check when the different sources were written or produced and by whom. Now decide which source you think is more reliable and why.

*Example*: Maybe some sources disagree on the name of a regional cuisine or whether or not a specific local cuisine is important. Maybe they disagree on what the main dishes are in that area. How do you decide which information is more reliable? Perhaps some of your sources are more up to date, or the person behind it spent more time in China or has a more extensive understanding of food and culture. Choosing to rely on the right sources is very important.

4) Use the data you gathered to draw a map or make a relevant graph. A visualization of the data helps us gain a deeper understanding of its context and wider meaning.

*Example*: Take a map of all of China and divide it according to local cuisine. Be as accurate as you can in dividing the country up. Another option is to make a graph of the most popular foods in the country divided by region. The exact content of the visualization matters less than the decisions that go into the representation and the deeper understanding of visual stimulation.

5) Create a narrative based on your research. Take an element in your research that particularly interested you and tell the full story about it. Try to make the story as interesting and appealing as possible.

*Example*: When you went through the sources, was there a story or piece of information stuck with you? Perhaps there was an individual, region, or dish with a fascinating origin? What was so interesting about it? Look further into that story and develop it. Put together the narrative to interest even people who are not interested in Chinese cuisine.

TV Show Analysis

Are you about to start binge-watching a TV show? Of course, you are. Many people think of TV as a waste of time. But a show with a strong plot and interesting characters excites our minds to think critically. We often wonder, what motivated the character to act that way? Why was this character killed off? Was it because of plot-related reasons or production reasons? What will happen next? What would I have done if I was in that position?

If we focus on these questions, they can be an avenue to very useful exercises in critical thinking. Next time you start a new show, use it as an opportunity to engage in the following critical thinking exercise.

1) After watching 2-3 episodes, write down a list of the show's main characters. Give a general sketch of the characteristics of each one. What motivates them? Why do they act the way they do? Every time the writers add a new and important character, update your list.

2) At the end of every episode, write down how the characters behaved in that episode. Compare it to your initial analysis of the characters' motivations. Was the behavior of the character predictable? Did it surprise you? When a character surprises you, ask yourself: why? Was the writing inconsistent, did the character change, or was there always more to the character than met the eye?

3) When you reach the end of each season, think about each character's social implications. Does the character represent any wider social issues of class, race, politics, ethics, or any other category you can think of? Is the representation intentional? Is the representation fair? Does it come at the expense of the story, or does it serve the narrative?

4) Once you finish the show, compare your initial impressions of the characters with what you thought of them first. Was your initial assessment of their motivation accurate? Are you surprised at how their story turned out or was it expected? Is there social significance to the characters' fate, or was the writer focused on the narrative?

These exercises are a fun way to develop some of the main elements of critical thinking. You can learn to structure research questions, gather data, create visual and verbal narratives, even while taking part in seemingly silly activities such as these.

## News Review

We have never had more sources of news available to us. Social media has exposed us to a variety of information or disinformation disguised as news. However, a great deal of it is simply untrustworthy. Some of it is based on fact but very biased in one direction or another. Another problem is that facts and opinions are often presented interchangeably as reliable news.

It is important to differentiate between fact, opinion, and disinformation. With this exercise, we can further our ability to do so while improving our critical thinking skills.

The news stories will include at least one of the following elements:

1) *Facts*: these are bits of true information and can be proven based on specific information or data.

2) *Opinion*: a point of view based on a conception of how the world works and how it should work. Meanwhile, an opinion is a point of view based on facts but ultimately cannot be proven right or wrong.

3) *Disinformation*: bits of information masquerading as facts, which you can disprove based on specific information or data.

Exercise: Next time you find yourself very interested in an event making headlines, do the following.

1) Gather five articles on the topic. One from a news source you use regularly. Two from sources you dislike and two from sources you do not know or have no opinion on.

2) Read one of the articles carefully and rate each one from 1 to 10 along with the following metrics: how accurate are the stories? How interesting are they to read? How agreeable do you find the positions?

3) List how many important and relevant facts are in each story. Write them down and cross-reference the facts. Are there facts that appear in all the stories? Are there facts that appear in most stories? Are there facts that only appear in one?

4) Now, make a list of each important fact regardless of the source. Give each fact a grade (A being 100% accurate and F being a shameless lie) based on the following metrics:

- Can this fact be proven without a doubt?
- If it can be, is it verified and based on data? What is the source of the data? Is it reliable?
- Is there a clear bias in the presentation of facts?
- Is it presented misleadingly? Are there important elements missing that you may have seen in some of the other stories?
- Are there opinions masquerading as facts?
- Are there bits of "information" masquerading as facts? Are there bits of information mentioned here which other stories convincingly debunk?

5) Now assign the facts back to the articles you found them in. Which articles are based mostly on facts graded B and above? Which have a bunch of falsehoods?

6) Now compare the article's factuality with the ratings you gave each article in step 2. How do they compare? Did any sources surprise you in their accuracy? Did any surprise you with their inaccuracy?

You may be surprised to see that some of the more trusted sources are inaccurate in certain ways and vice versa.

This exercise serves as a reminder that we evaluate all information fairly. Some information sources are more trustworthy than others, but all information should be verified and analyzed critically.

## Action Steps

I have actively filled this chapter with practical and (hopefully) fun action steps you can take to improve your critical thinking. Remember, you should not just read this last chapter. You should practice it! You can increase your critical thinking skills by completing these exercises carefully and thoroughly. They are all designed for you to use repeatedly, so redo them if you can!

You may find repetitive tasks annoying, but there are good reasons for you to do so. Studies have shown that explaining the concept of critical thinking to individuals is important. However, it does little on its own.

To truly internalize the concept, it is crucial to engage in critical thinking regularly. Learning how to think critically in principle without acting on it is a bit like reading about going to the gym. Sure, it can prepare you somewhat for the experience, but it does precious little to get us in shape.

## Conclusion

This chapter provided you with a blueprint of fun exercises we designed to help improve your critical thinking. If you feel like you have benefited from these exercises, make up your own! You know what interests you better than we do, so you are guaranteed to come up with even better exercises.

If you use critical thinking every time you read the news or watch TV, it won't be long before you reach those 10,000 hours of expertise. And you will get to catch up on your favorite shows while you do it.

# AFTERWORD

In his later days, Nikola Tesla earned a reputation as a complete madman. Some of his ideas do sound incredibly far-fetched. He had a plan to harness all human energy from outer space. Another plan he was working on was to construct a massive ring worldwide, allowing you to travel around the planet in 24 hours.

It also didn't help that he was celibate, measured the volume of all the food he ate, and did not practice basic hygiene.

However, only today are we beginning to appreciate the full magnitude of his brilliance. He invented and perfected the science behind the mass use of electricity. Indeed, he was fired by Thomas Edison for refusing to work through his preferred electrical system. His later writings predicted wi-fi internet, among other things. When Tesla died, he had 300 patents to his name. He was also greatly maligned and penniless.

Though people at the time may have thought he was bizarre, Tesla redefined science in his time by questioning everything. He went with the well-reasoned and researched truth; social consequences be damned.

We designed this book to help you think critically and plan better solutions for your problems. However, this is not a theoretical book. We also intended it to help you apply these solutions in real-life situations.

We have tried to focus on bringing out that inner Tesla in all of us. As critical thinkers, we question the world around us and gather evidence to back up all of our claims. We then create well-reasoned solutions to the problems around us and use the foresight we have gained in the process to predict future problems. Throughout, we adapt our plans to changing circumstances on the ground.

However, we also wish to avoid Tesla's ultimate fate. As we discussed later in this book, we must actively adapt our plans and solutions to appeal to those around us. To this end, we have discussed how to cultivate critical thought in different arenas and "sell" our products to other individuals.

Now you are ready to use these skills in all of the areas of your life. Remember to use these skills judiciously. Life is a marathon and not a sprint. Not every small decision requires the application of the full critical thought process. If you use it too often, you will also develop fatigue.

However, make sure to apply it to every important decision you make. If properly applied, it will save you from so many preventable mistakes. It will also make your life and the lives of those around you better. If you solve your problems like Tesla but market your solutions like Coca Cola, you will get far.

## ONE FINAL WORD FROM US

If this book has helped you in any way, we'd appreciate it if you left a review on Amazon. Reviews are the lifeblood of our business. We read every single one and incorporate your feedback in developing future book projects.

To leave a review, simply go to: smarturl.it/ctianr

(Or scan the code with your camera)

## CONTINUING YOUR JOURNEY

> **Those Who Keep Learning, Will Keep Rising In Life.**
>
> — Charlie Munger (Billionaire, Investor, and Warren Buffet's Business Partner)

The most successful people in life are those who enjoy learning and asking questions, understanding themselves and the world around them.

In our Thinknetic newsletter we'll share with you our best thinking improvement tips and tricks to help you become even more successful in life.

It's 100% free and you can unsubscribe at any time.

Besides, you'll hear first about our new releases and get the chance to receive them for free or highly discounted.

As a bonus, you'll get 2 thinking improvement sheets completely for free.

**Go to thinknetic.net to sign up for free!**

(Or simply scan the code with your camera)

# THE TEAM BEHIND THINKNETIC

**Michael Meisner, Founder and CEO**

When Michael got into publishing books on Amazon, he found that his favorite topic - the thinking process and its results, is tackled in a much too complex and unengaging way. Thus, he set himself up to make his ideal a reality: books that are informative, entertaining, and can help people achieve success by thinking things through.

This ideal became his passion and profession. He built a team of like-minded people and is in charge of the strategic part and brand orientation, as he continues to improve and extend his business.

**Diana Spoiala, Publishing Manager**

From idea to print, there is a process involving researching and designing the book, writing and editing it, and providing it with the right covers. Diana oversees this process and ensures the quality of each book. Outside work, she dedicates most of her time cultivating her innate love for reading and writing literature, poetry, and philosophy.

## Theresa Datinguinoo, Research and Outline Mastermind

Theresa derives "immense satisfaction from putting together ideas to provide a solid framework for an engaging story and seeing the final product come to life." Her professional background is in human resources management and psychology, but she has always enjoyed writing articles and blog posts about any subject.

## Doris Lam, Senior Content Editor

Doris has been editing print media since 2005 as the Chief Copy Editor and Program Coordinator for several environmental agencies. She is committed to helping writers achieve clarity, always up for the challenge of making everyone's writing a masterpiece. For more information about Doris's great work, visit www.dorissiu.com.

## Nerina Badalic, Senior Content Editor

Throughout the years, Nerina wrote articles, short stories, and songs. As an editor, she helps authors bring out the best in them to produce manuals, thesis, articles, and books that are valuable and useful to the readers. Nerina continues to explore the arts that surround the world of words: communication, marketing, design, music, and photography.

## Francesca Scotti-Goetz, Newsletter Writer and Social Media Community Manager

An observer first and a copywriter second, Francesca has a passion for the intersection of art with humanity; social issues with media; thinking with creativity. She spends her weekends in Amsterdam with a camera and a notebook, and her weekdays harnessing her discoveries to effectively engage with Thinknetic's worldwide community.

## Contributors:

## David Brant Yu

David is committed to carefully reviewing the profiles of the many aspiring writers for Thinknetic, ensuring that the most skilled and talented ones join the team. His voracious reading habit and interests in philosophy and current affairs help him carry out his work critically. David enjoys his spare time doing freelance copyediting and English tutoring.

## Evangeline Obiedo

Evangeline completes our books' journey to getting published. She pays attention to all the details, making sure that every book is properly formatted. Her love for learning extends into the real world - she loves traveling and experiencing new places and cultures.

# REFERENCES

## 1. What Is Critical Thinking?

1. Gill, C. (1973) 'The Death of Socrates,' The Classic Quarterly, 23(1), pp. 25-28. Doi: https://www.jstor.org/stable/638122
2. Mintz, A. (2005) 'From grade school to law school: Socrates' legacy in education,' in A companion to Socrates. New York: Riley, pp. 476-492.
3. Hawkins-Leon, C. (1998) 'The Socratic Method-Problem Method Dichotomy, Brigham Young University Education and Law Journal, 1998(1-2), pp. 1-18.
4. Anderson, G. and Piro, J. (2014) 'Conversations in Socrates café: scaffolding critical-thinking via Socratic questioning and dialogues,' *New Horizons for Learning*, 11(1), pp. 1-9. doi: 10.1080/01626620.2015.1048.009.
5. Epsey, M. (2018) 'Enhancing critical thinking using team-based learning,' *Higher Education Research and Development*, 37(1), pp. 15-29. doi: 10.1080/07294360.2017.1344196
6. Dwyer, C. Boswell, A. and Elliott, M. (2015) 'An evaluation of critical-thinking competencies in business settings,' *Journal of Education for Business*, 90(5), pp. 260-269. doi: 10.1080/08832323.2015.1038978.
7. Facione, P.A. (1990) '*The Delphi report: executive summary*'. California: The California Academic Press, pp. 315 423.
8. Vandenberg, D. (2013) 'Critical thinking about truth in teaching: the epistemic ethos,' *Educational Philosophy and Theory*, 41(2), pp. 155-165. doi: https://doi.org/10.1111/j.1469-5812.2007.00393.x.
9. Christensen, C.; M Raynor, and McDonald, R. (2015) "What Is Disruptive Innovation?" *Harvard Business Review*, 93 (12), pp. 44–53.
10. Ritala, P.; Golnam, A.; Wegmann, A. (2014) 'Coopetition-based business models: The case of Amazon.com,' *Industrial Marketing Management*, 43(2), pp. 236-249.
11. Inch, E. and Tudor, K. (2013) '*Critical thinking and communication: The use of reason in argument.*' New York: Pearson.

12. Paul, R. (1993) 'The Logic of Creative and Critical Thinking,' *American Behavioral Scientist*, 37(1), pp. 21-39. doi: 10.1177/0002764293037001004
13. Hundleby, C. (2010) 'The Authority of the Fallacies Approach to Argument Evaluation," *Informal Logic*, 20(3), pp. 279-308. doi: 10.22329/il.v30i3.3035
14. Elliott, B.; Oty, K.; McArthur, J. and Clark, B.; (2010) 'The effect of an interdisciplinary algebra/science course on students' problem solving skills, critical thinking skills and attitudes towards mathematics," *International Journal of Mathematical Education in Science and Technology*, 32(6), pp. 811-816. doi: 10.1080/00207390110053784

# 2. Critical Thinking Framework: Understanding The Elements And Steps Needed For Critical Thinking

1. Paul, R. and Elder, L. (2006) '*Critical thinking tools for taking charge of your learning and your life.*' New Jersey: Prentice Hall Publishing.
2. Paul, R. and Elder, L. (2006) '*Critical thinking tools for taking charge of your learning and your life.*' New Jersey: Prentice Hall Publishing.
3. Jackson, S. (2011) '*Research methods and statistics: a critical thinking approach.*' New York: Wadsworth.
4. Jackson, S. (2011) '*Research methods and statistics: a critical thinking approach.*' New York: Wadsworth.
5. Pickard, M. (2007) 'The New Bloom's Taxonomy,' *Journal of Family and Consumer Sciences Education*, 25(1), pp. 45-55. doi: doi: 10.22099/jtls.2012.336
6. Bloom, B.S., Engelhart, M.D., Furst, E.J., Hill, W.H. and Krathwohl, D.R. (1956). Taxonomy of educational objectives: the classification of educational goals. In '*Handbook I:cognitive domain.*' New York: David McKay.
7. Krathwohl, D. (2002) 'A revision of Bloom's taxonomy: an overview,' *Theory Into Practice*, 41(4), pp. 212-218. doi: 10.1207/s15430421tip4104_2.

## 3. The Evolution Of A Critical Mind: What Sets Critical Thinkers Apart

1. Blumer, A.; et al. (1987) 'Occam's Razor,' *Information Processing Letters*, 24(6), pp. 377-380. doi:10.1016/0020-0190(87)90114-1
2. Linker, M. (2014) '*Intellectual empathy: critical thinking for social justice.*' Ann Arbor, MI: University of Michigan Press.
3. Li-Fang, Z. (2010) 'Thinking styles and the big five personality traits,' *Educational Psychology*, 22(10), pp. 17-31. doi: 10.1080/01443410120101224.

## 4. Barriers To Critical Thinking

1. Connell-Carrick, K. (2006) 'Trends in popular parenting books and the need for parental critical thinking,' *Child Welfare*, 85(5), pp. 819-836. doi: https://eric.ed.gov/?id=EJ745853.
2. Edward, D. (2005) 'Confusion of a necessary with a sufficient condition,' in *Attacking Faulty Reasoning*. Boston, MA: Wadsworth Publishing, pp. 151.
3. Edward, D. (2005) 'Confusion of a necessary with a sufficient condition,' in *Attacking Faulty Reasoning*. Boston, MA: Wadsworth Publishing, pp. 151.
4. Gooden, D. and Zenker, F. (2015) 'Denying antecedents and affirming consequents: the state of the art,' *Informal Logic*, 35(1), pp. 88-134. doi: 10.22329/il.v35i1.4173.
5. Ennis, R. (1998) 'Is critical thinking culturally biased?' *Teaching Philosophy*, 21(1), pp. 15-33. doi: 10.5840/teachphil19982113.
6. Haber, J. (2020) '*Critical thinking.*' Cambridge, MA: MIT University Press.

## 5. Ready, Set, Go: Applying Critical Thinking To Your Personal And Professional Life

1. Tversky, A. and Kahneman, D. (1974) 'Judgment under uncertainty: heuristics and biases,' *Science*, 185(4157), pp. 1124-1131. doi: http://www.jstor.org/stable/1738360.
2. World Food Program, "*Overview*," United Nations World Food Program. doi: https://www.wfp.org/overview

3. Park, W.W. (1990) 'A Review of research on Groupthink,' *Behavioral Decision Making*, 3(4), pp. 229-245. doi: https://doi.org/10.1002/bdm.3960030402